FROM THE INSIDE OF THE
KEYHOLE

FROM THE INSIDE OF THE KEYHOLE

CHALLENGING A DIAGNOSIS OF MANIC DEPRESSION
(BIPOLAR DISORDER)

MARGARET A. GRIFFITHS

authorHOUSE®

AuthorHouse™
1663 Liberty Drive
Bloomington, IN 47403
www.authorhouse.com
Phone: 1-800-839-8640

© 2012 by Margaret A. Griffiths. All rights reserved.

No part of this book may be reproduced, stored in a retrieval system, or transmitted by any means without the written permission of the author.

Published by AuthorHouse   May 2012

ISBN: 978-1-4772-3797-7 (sc)
ISBN: 978-1-4772-3798-4 (hc)
ISBN: 978-1-4772-3799-1 (e)

Any people depicted in stock imagery provided by Thinkstock are models, and such images are being used for illustrative purposes only.
Certain stock imagery © Thinkstock.

This book is printed on acid-free paper.

Because of the dynamic nature of the Internet, any web addresses or links contained in this book may have changed since publication and may no longer be valid. The views expressed in this work are solely those of the author and do not necessarily reflect the views of the publisher, and the publisher hereby disclaims any responsibility for them.

To my Dear Friend,

Hope you enjoy my first book of the series.

Love Mary
xx

To Benjamin, the Olivers, and Elizabeth

Epigraph

You are a child of the universe,
no less than the trees and the stars;
you have a right to be here.
And whether or not it is clear to you,
no doubt the universe is unfolding as it should.

Therefore, be at peace with God,
whatever you conceive Him to be,
and whatever your labors and aspirations,
in the noisy confusion of life,
keep peace with your soul.

With all its sham, drudgery and broken dreams,
it is still a beautiful world.
Be careful. Strive to be happy.

Desiderata by Max Ehrmann 1927

CONTENTS

Epigraph vii

Foreword xi

Preface xiii

Introduction xv

Part 1: *Fighting the Diagnosis—the Consequences* 1

Part 2: *Accepting the Diagnosis—the Consequences* 57

Part 3: *Victory over the Consequences* 97

Afterword: *Unravelling the Mystery* 121

About the Author 131

Foreword

There were many paths Margy could have gone down in her life. Nearly all of them, with few exceptions, would have led to self-destruction. She did come close to ending her life when the torment she had to endure was too much. However, in spite of it all, she didn't choose the typical escape route of alcohol and other 'recreational' drugs. Margy dug deep and rose above it all to achieve an extraordinary outcome.

It dawned on me the other day just how far she has come. We were talking about her upcoming adventure (to live overseas with her husband, Ben) and previous journeys abroad. Here is someone who had her teens and twenties stolen from her through cruel circumstance—a genetic time bomb that went off when triggered by family dysfunction and then was exacerbated by misdirected love and health care bureaucracy. Yet she was able to battle great odds to finish high school and get a university degree. She then went on to influence many people throughout her career and life in a very positive way.

Such is her giving nature that, after all she has been through, she chose to relive the pain and write this book so others might gain insight into this mental health enigma. Margy has shut the door to her painful past firmly behind her and is now living a life that is an inspiration to us all. She has shown what is possible if you have absolute belief in yourself.

Love you forever, Sis.
Bobby

PREFACE

They sye that time 'eals all things,
They sye you can always forget;
But the smiles an' the tears across the years,
They twist my 'eart-strings yet! [1*]

The words of this song capture the essence of my life after I was diagnosed with 'manic depressive psychosis' forty-one years ago. Subsequent changes in the terminology used to describe this condition—'affective disorder', 'mood disorder', and, currently, 'bipolar disorder'—did nothing to help me unravel the maze in which I found myself.

Maybe you have recently been diagnosed with this condition, or maybe a friend or member of your family has. This is a critical time during which hope battles with despair.

In the following pages, I would like to share with you the insights I have gained into the diagnosis and treatment of manic depression, and the happy lifestyle that may emerge.

It is not based solely on the clinician's professional viewpoint, observation, and treatment of the patient. It shows the reactions and reasoning of the individual confronted by a new world in which fear, anxiety, and distortions of reality play a prominent part.

The name of my book, *From the Inside of the Keyhole*, derives from a concept formed during meditation whilst I was secluded in a locked room as part of a treatment programme. This idea was reinforced during subsequent hospitalizations.

In this book, I will illustrate the strong influence of parental input on the diagnosis and subsequent treatment regime, plus the devastating effects of psychiatric medication.

I have travelled a long road with many 'smiles an' tears', but the distance I needed to travel was only short by comparison to this. *From the Inside of the Keyhole* offers the hope that, no matter how difficult your

---

[1] * Song in George Orwell's *Nineteen Eighty-Four*, a novel published in 1949.

situation or how dismal your perspective, you can still rise above it all by maintaining belief in yourself.

The setting is mainly in Australia, in my hometown of Ipswich and the surrounding areas including Brisbane, the capital of Queensland, approximately twenty miles away. There are short periods in Singapore and Hong Kong, but the universal nature of psychiatric treatment makes my message relevant on a global basis.

From the Inside of the Keyhole incorporates direct transcripts of my treatment taken from notes made available to me through the Freedom of Information Act. I will label quotes in this book so obtained 'FOI Notes'. As such, my maiden name of Oliver appears in some of these transcripts. In the text I have substituted names for doctors and friends to protect their privacy. Family names as well as the names of the various hospitals and locations are unchanged.

Let me open some of the doors of my life—step inside, see how it feels. Assess the situation . . . enjoy the humour and the irony. Maybe you'll see yourself through these pages—as a patient, a parent, a friend, or a doctor.

You may also understand why I felt it so necessary to challenge the diagnosis of manic depression after much contemplation 'from the inside of the keyhole' and beyond.

Introduction

'I see. Thank you,' he said, putting down the phone. 'Well, your level is 7.6. That's good. What was it last time?'

'I'm not sure. My last test was four months ago.'

And so, the low-key, casual conversation continued between Dr Sorensen, 'shrink', and me. The topic under discussion was the level of lithium carbonate present in my bloodstream as shown in a serum lithium test.

The remarkable factor highlighted here is the simple, non-pressured, non-threatening consultation. As Dr Sorensen flicked through his clinical notes, looking for the previous test results, my mind turned back the pages of time . . .

Other offices and other doctors paraded before me—glimpses from the past . . . a past that I often felt was best left in the shadows of dim memories. This same past, which I thought I had dealt with so thoroughly and had been able to view in the best positive light, could still tear me apart if I decided to dwell on the negative aspects.

These aspects were not necessarily the worst things that had happened to me, or the worst things I had done, but the suffering and pain that could have, and should have, been avoided for all concerned in the diagnosis, explanation, and acceptance of this illness.

For myself, this understanding and subsequent acceptance did not occur until seventeen years after my initial diagnosis, whilst I was listening to a talk-back radio programme led by a psychiatrist. After I had been listening for about year, a last caller queried the cause of manic depression. That evening the psychiatrist outlined a theory that explained the reasons for the occurrence of manic depression, stating it was caused by a gene that had the propensity to trigger its onset. Any event, good or bad, that caused a big emotional response could activate this gene. He further related that this gene might skip a generation or go sideways in a family.

At that time, this was a theory I could believe in, identify with, and accept. I was elated! It was not until then that I was able to consider the appropriate treatment in a positive light.

I was brought out of my reverie when Dr Sorensen asked me to confirm how many tablets of lithium carbonate I was taking a day. This was really a reversal in itself, for the doctor to ask the patient. I told him that I was taking six per day. It was at this point I took the initiative. I asked Dr Sorensen if he would halve my lithium dose, which would lessen the intensity of possible side effects on my kidneys and thyroid gland, yet still be within reach of a quick build up should I need it.

Happily, almost unbelievably, he agreed to a reduction to four tablets a day. This was not until 1993, and this step marked the beginning of a real turnaround for my health.

It had not always been so easy to communicate my feelings and my needs.

PART 1

Fighting the Diagnosis—the Consequences

Chapter 1

This was the night I would always remember.

I was thirteen years old. I had woken softly from sleep in my still-darkened bedroom and wondered what time it was. As if in answer to my silent query, the dull chimes of the mantle clock in the lounge room sounded twelve times—twelve ominous strikes, as I was to reflect later.

Through my thoughts filtered the sound of voices coming from my parents' room across the hallway. 'It's the time of the Second Coming. Rev Jones knows about it, and he will be so excited he won't be able to sleep either.' My mother's voice was low and intense but clearly audible in the still of the night. My father was silent after this revelation.

My mother continued, 'I have to tell you something—a confession that will save Margaret and Robert. You will have to confess anything too.'

She then began a very detailed account of a relationship she had had when my father was working in another state. She told him every most intimate detail, none of which was meant for my ears. I listened in shock and surprise for a little while. My father was very kind and understanding, I thought, telling her he was a man of the world and that some woman had shown interest in him whilst he was away.

I did not want to hear any more, so I called out that I was going to get a glass of water. I thought they would stop talking if they knew I was awake.

I had my drink, but as I was coming back, my mother was up and met me in the lounge room. She grabbed me and held me very tight, and my father said to her, 'Let her go. You'll choke her!'

But she didn't let go, and she screamed out, 'Oh, God, if this is hell, let me die!'

I don't think she meant to hurt me, but she was crushing me to her in her anguish. Father pulled us apart, and my mother made a strange statement that seemed out of context to the whole situation. Looking at me, she said, 'Something happened to me, once, that was so bad, I'll never tell anyone. I'll take it to the grave with me.'

Then Father took her back to bed, but I don't think anyone slept any more that night except maybe my brother, who was only eight at the time and doesn't recall these events.

Mother had always attended church, and my brother and I went to Sunday school. So the next morning we took Mother to see her minister, Rev Jones, who was unable to comfort or help her.

The family then went to my grandmother's place, which we did every weekend, but Mother was becoming more and more disorientated. She lay in bed talking to people who weren't there, and I sat on the bed beside her and stroked her hair for a long time.

As I sat beside her, I was thinking to myself how lovely she had been looking lately and how young she seemed, even though she had already turned fifty.

Now here she was in this very distressed state. I felt very sorry for her, and very sorry for Father in the light of what I had overheard.

I think my father was hoping she would begin to improve and get back to normal given a little time, but when she continued to be so confused, he asked my cousin Liz, who was a nurse, if she would go with Mother to the Royal Brisbane Hospital, approximately twenty miles away.

I don't know why he didn't take her himself, but Liz went with her in the train, and said she was very relieved when they finally arrived as my mother had been very unsettled, wanting to leave the train all the time.

Mother was admitted to the psyche ward, Lowson House, where she stayed for several weeks. She underwent shock treatment at her own desperate request, although Father wasn't happy she had given permission for this.

In the meantime, our grandmother came to stay. As she had only recently broken both her wrists, it fell upon my father, my brother, and me, to look after the household and keep things running smoothly.

Also unbeknown to me was the genetic heritage I was carrying. I had heard about a distant cousin who was supposed to have had 'melancholia', but this hadn't seemed to me to have any relevance on my life.

Only later did different fragments of this cloth emerge—I discovered facts that had been kept hidden from me, and secrets concealed by the passage of time and distance, which proved very difficult to unravel. Cryptic clues came up now and then, which I found intriguing.

For instance, on one occasion when Mother was home again, we were talking about her distress before she went to hospital, and she remarked, 'When the ambulance came, I thought it was a hearse. I thought I was dead.' Then she added, 'I wished I was dead.' Only on later reflection did I remember that she hadn't gone to hospital in an ambulance. Yet she seemed so focused and so adamant in this memory. Was there a previous event she was referring to? And just what was it all about? I must admit I was very curious and found it very interesting to say the least.

But not once in all that time did I ever think any less of her for what had happened, and not once did I have anything but good feelings for her. I never mentioned what I had heard on that fateful night to anyone. In fact, it would not come up in the context of this story if it hadn't ricocheted into my own life just over two years later.

My mother sought solace in religion and believed she found comfort there, although she never really learnt to forgive herself, or to trust others to do the right thing in their personal lives.

When my mother first came out of hospital, every day was a real battle for her, and we all used to try and encourage her.

As you may appreciate, a mother in this fragile state ceases to be available to answer ordinary, everyday questions about growing up. I became anxious that my body was not developing in a womanly enough shape, and I reasoned that if I lost a little weight, I would look in better proportion.

So I began to cut down on food and to exercise a lot. This progressed to the stage where I was eating very little and even taking food off my plate and putting it onto my lap to get rid of it later. Plus I was exercising nearly constantly. I lost approximately five kilos (about eleven pounds)—not all that dramatic, really, but then I got the idea that I was too skinny, and reversed the process and started eating more and more till I did become noticeably overweight. I had allowed myself to believe that my weight now decided my feelings and my attitude, although previously it hadn't even concerned me.

Just as all of this was happening, I was becoming more and more downhearted, so much so that after being in the top five of my class consistently, and averaging 95 per cent, I felt unable to attend school or study—or do anything.

In a very short time, I had become a 'problem', and sensible reasoning went out the window. My parents blamed my dieting for the way I was feeling, and I began to accept this link myself. I visited a doctor at the local hospital, and he put me on antidepressants.

Finally, I returned to school after missing a whole term in my junior year. I was not on any medication, and everything quickly started falling back into place—my grades were only in the low seventies when I first returned, but I brought them up and received a scholarship in my junior certificate.

I was in the school band, had my first boyfriend, and I was happy. My whole family seemed happy, but things were changing regarding the way my parents interpreted even the simple things I did.

This was the turning point of everyone's emotions and feelings towards each other. I never understood why, but after my mother admitted her indiscretion, it seemed that I was to become the focus of discontent and suspicion. The period that followed acted as a barrier that locked out progress and opportunities for many years to come.

Chapter 2

'Well, young lady, why do you think you've been brought here?' queried the elderly, heavily moustached, local police sergeant.

'I don't know. My parents have been busy talking, making something immoral or outrageous out of nothing.'

As my parents tried to interject, the officer continued, 'Well, tell me in your own words what happened this afternoon.'

'All right. I was home by myself when Jeremy, a friend of mine from school, dropped in. He'd been off sick from school for a long time, and Dad used to take me around to his home to visit him—' My father interrupted angrily to say that his parents were always there during those visits.

'Anyway,' I continued, 'we listened to some music on the stereo, and I cooked him some spaghetti for lunch. We were going to ride our bikes up to the Olympic pool and have a swim. Just before we left, Dad rang up and said a neighbour had told him I had a boy there, and he didn't like it. I told him who it was and that we going up to the pool. We were halfway up to the pool when Dad drove up behind us and followed us in his car all the way to the pool. I couldn't believe it! Then, when I arrived home, he was in a real rage, and my parents brought me here.'

After listening to my story, the officer remained unconvinced of any impropriety and suggested to my parents that maybe they could buy me a dog for company, like the little one that had sat on the floor next to him during this interview. No doubt this wasn't the response my parents were expecting.

It was the August school holidays. I was fifteen and a half. I just couldn't understand this change in my father's attitude—and that was only the beginning. From that time onwards, everything became a major issue. It didn't matter what the situation was, there was some connotation put on it, and for what reason, I couldn't imagine.

This home environment of hostility and distrust continued to grow. It was during this year that my mother returned twice to hospital for further psychiatric treatment. Once again, it fell to me to take over the cooking, cleaning, and general housework. When my mother returned from hospital, I was once again under the microscope.

I composed a poem titled 'Respect', which pretty well summed up my feelings at this time—for my family and the world as a whole.

Respect

How often we hear this word mentioned,
How often we're told to respect—
But just what do they mean when they tell us?
Do they mean to just blindly accept?

When they give us their ideas so biased,
By old times and things long ago,
When they were the 'poor, suppressed children',
Who never were given a go!

But now things are different they tell us,
We're cheeky, facetious; we're bad!
We ne'er even try to please them,
They say that we're driving them mad!

But is this the truth?
Are they facing the facts?
Have they the right to pass judgement?
Do they really know all?
Can they never be wrong?
Ne'er listening to reason or wherefore!

Each day they condemn us,
But are we to blame?
They say that our attitude,
Is causing them shame!

Our attitude! Our attitude!!
They hammer this home.
But what is our attitude?
How do we feel?

What have we done?
And also, 'What's real?'

Look at the hippies, the addicts, the thugs,
The poor desperate people now taking drugs.
The riots, the fighting,
The lust just to kill.
Are we to blame?
Must we take the bill?

Population explosions!
Who can they blame?
Not us, but take it out on us just the same!

Now who is it taught us of killing and crime?
Who gave us lessons in fear and in dread?
Who jokingly threatened us 'We'd have to go!'
Who is it told us that they 'didn't know!'
Know what? What we would do or degenerate to?
Know what would happen, to us their beloved?

Of course it's our parents—
Wise, wonderful them!
They've taught us these things,
And we've learnt them so well!

We know that they love us,
But how do they show us?
By sarcastic remarks,
And 'fear for our welfare'?

They show us their lives,
What a mess they have made.
But now they are wiser—
They want us to save!

But what of their method?
This is the thing.

Their attitude also,
Could maybe take blame.

What be the right way?
What can they do?
How can they show us
To be loving and true?

By turning to Jesus,
To God—Yes it's true!
This is the way out,
The only way too!

But no, they won't listen,
They won't change their ways.
They're better than us—
And that's how they'll stay!

    I liked talking to people, helping them if I could, and at this time, I regularly attended church. I had also become reasonably attractive and was enjoying the small attentions boys were beginning to give me.

    It was while I was sixteen that I met Joel, who came to mean a great deal to me. I just lived for the days to arrive on which I was due to see him. Things seemed to be going smoothly, or so I thought, with no specific warning of what was to follow. My parents became very protective and anxious for my well-being, and very suspicious of me and any of my real or imagined actions.

    This resulted in an atmosphere so sparked with tension and threats of violence, that I came to dread my return home from school in the afternoons. I was cross-examined on anything I said or did, and so were my friends. Apparently all my actions were suspect, and my parents seemed to think it was their duty to protect me from myself. As a consequence, I became very unhappy and distraught. My life was unbearable.

    Looking back, I can see that my father had become a very worried man. He had a very unstable wife and, supposedly, a very difficult daughter. My brother told me many years later of the very negative impact that all of this disturbance and unrest had on his life.

Suffice to say that, by the time I was just over sixteen years old, I couldn't understand or handle my home situation at all. Over the phone, I secured a job as a nanny for two children. I would live with the family, as the parents were both working.

Telling only some neighbours with whom I was friendly, and a minister of religion who was also my friend, I disappeared from my home leaving no forwarding address.

Chapter 3

No doubt, many parents reading of this, would be familiar with a similar pattern of events, and would see it all from the parents' viewpoint, and understand the dismay and unbearable distress that similar behaviour to mine could cause.

On the other hand, many 'rebellious' kids would recognize this situation as one from which escape seemed the only solution.

For myself, being liberated as a nanny was a great feeling! Being treated as a family member in a considerate manner, and being appreciated bolstered up my self-esteem, which had been suffering badly.

One evening, I received a phone call from my minister friend telling me my parents knew where I was and were coming down to get me.

When my parents arrived, late in the evening, they were hostile and abusive to my new family. They asked all sorts of blatant questions trying to establish that I was leading some sort of immoral lifestyle. Although they received no substantiation of this, they still had their own agenda.

Because I, to quote their own words, had 'made fools of them', they were interested in salvaging their pride. Instead of coming to any form of reconciliation, they were interested in 'taking me to the police, seeing if I was pregnant, and having me referred to a psychiatric hospital.'

A friend of my father's had driven them down to my new address and was very sympathetic to my position. He tried to tone down these feelings, and even suggested taking the whole family down to the Gold Coast for the weekend and making a fresh start.

However, that was out of the question.

The following morning, early, I was taken directly to the police station and then to a doctor who wrote a letter of referral for my admission to Lowson House, the same locked psyche ward my mother had attended.

Once there, I underwent a comprehensive series of psychological tests. Soon after, I had a short interview with the head psychiatrist and a room full of medical students. I resented their unnecessary presence and insinuations, and was rewarded for my calm presentation and subdued anger with a diagnosis of 'manic depressive psychosis'. I was completely taken aback by this result—it was so ludicrous and unrealistic. I could not accept it at all!

In fact, it fitted in very well with a trend that had developed with my parents by that time—if they weren't happy with something I'd done, it was not because I was defiant or wrong. It was because I was 'sick'. How convenient!

My stance of fighting against this diagnosis was to provide the perfect ammunition to seal my fate—no doubt, a perfect 'Catch 22' situation.

I was in hospital for three weeks, placed on a regime of lithium carbonate, and released into my father's protective custody on condition I attended follow-up visits to the psychiatric outpatient's section of the Ipswich General Hospital.

My parents were adamant in wanting me to return to school and finish my senior certificate. By contrast, I felt it was the end of the world that I'd been put in a psychiatric hospital, and I didn't want to be the subject of discussion and ridicule.

Before I left home, I'd been interested in training to be a cadet nurse. So I resumed this goal, and my parents, very reluctantly and after much debate, gave their permission.

Three weeks later, I was accepted as a cadet nurse at the same hospital where I had been diagnosed. Although I reached high standards in my year as a cadet nurse, interspersed over the months were periods when I questioned the accuracy of this diagnosis, and questioned the wisdom of taking lithium carbonate. This was mainly because I had been told when I began taking it that, 'It works because it slows down the body's reaction to the brain'.

The other problem I had with manic depression, or bipolar disorder, was the preconceived expectation that everyone had of it. It was automatically accepted that I would be sexually interested in everyone, that I would spend money recklessly, that I would be physically violent and dangerous, and that I would be psychotic. To my way of thinking, this was infinitely more damaging than a criminal record!

I was also extremely displeased to be having psychiatric medication forced upon me against my will. For all of these reasons, plus my own personal view of the illness as a stigma, I never mentioned my psychiatric history to anyone. My mother used to discuss it with everybody, and this also caused a lot of friction between us.

I didn't feel I had any of the so-called characteristics of manic depression, but after my diagnosis, it seemed everything I did was slotted into the condition's list of symptoms, in some context. The pattern had been set: if I did something my parents didn't approve of, they took refuge behind this illness and looked to treatment as a 'cure'.

Therefore, any of my attempts to get off lithium and lead a 'normal' life were counteracted by their cries for medication or hospitalization.

I had also been witness to the other poor souls at Lowson House who returned in a dazed and confused state from having shock treatment. This was completely new to me, but this was how I learned, in a very explicit manner, about the treatment my mother had endured.

My life in the nurses' quarters was filled with camaraderie, new friends, and nursing regulations. Living in the nurses' home as a cadet meant being in by eleven in the evening during weeknights and midnight on the weekends, and signing in and out on all occasions. This was more freedom than I could ever have envisaged, and life was good.

After a six-week induction study and practical course, we were introduced into the wards to learn from a more hands-on approach. Before each shift we reported to the senior sisters' office where we were scrutinized to ensure that our uniforms and personal grooming were at the correct standard.

I was still in touch with Joel, and I saw him once a week, but after nine months together we broke up after a misunderstanding. As we had been very close, I felt shattered by this, and very saddened, and this seriously upset the priorities I had laid down for myself. My weekend visits to the family continued.

At the conclusion of my course, the whole family, including my grandmother, went for a holiday to Hervey Bay. My brother enjoyed fishing and swimming, and I went on long walks with my dad. However, at the end of the three weeks, I felt more disillusioned than ever and did not return to continue training as a first-year nurse.

I attended an out-patients clinic at Ipswich General Hospital, where Dr Roberts put me on Tofranil (imipramine), a drug used to treat depression. He ceased my lithium saying it may have contributed to my feeling so low. It was at this clinic where I first met Dr Capella, who described my condition as 'depressed'.

I did not want to continue taking *any* medication, but my parents were in strong disagreement with this, and after much arguing and conflict, I agreed to go to Wolston Park Psychiatric Hospital, voluntarily, for assessment. However, as they were only interested in putting me on more medication, I signed myself out after three days.

As time passed, I started to feel a bit better, and I began, once again, to take an interest in things. No sooner had I started to feel improved and more positive, than my parents showed their disapproval and said I was 'high'.

There was a lot of tension at home, so I visited a local general practitioner, whom I trusted, and explained what was happening. Once again, I agreed to go to hospital voluntarily to try and sort everything out.

During this hospitalization, Dr Capella described me as 'over-talkative, overactive, and elated with pressure of speech and of thought.' (FOI Notes)

In fact, I was hypomanic!

Chapter 4

In a memorandum to the hospital superintendent, Dr Capella stated that, on my admission as a voluntary patient, because I had signed myself out on my previous visit, there was some doubt I would remain in hospital, so I was sent to Lowson House and returned two days later as a regulated patient. (FOI Notes)

As my readers can imagine, this could only serve to increase my agitation and hostility with the whole situation.

Dr Capella was a very patient man who spent a lot of time talking to me over this period. A social worker accompanied me home on a day's leave and reported back to Dr Capella on the family situation.

A month later, four days before I was scheduled to be discharged, a meeting was held with Dr Capella, the social worker, my parents, and me. According to the social worker, we were a very dysfunctional family in that my father never looked at me when he spoke to me, conveyed signals to my mother without saying anything, and was very controlling.

The social worker's report concluded: 'There appear to be several features of this family which have contributed to Margaret's illness. Firstly Margaret and her parents have quite divergent perceptions of her, particularly regarding her sexual behaviour. If these perceptions could be made more congruent, perhaps some of their destructive behaviour towards her would reduce. Although her parents claim she only behaves unusually during her manic and depressive phases, it is highly likely to me that their behaviour towards her would be quite destructive, even during her "normal" period.'

When he told my parents this, my father exploded and said, 'You are not going to blame *me* for this girl's behaviour! I will have her transferred to another doctor!' (FOI Notes)

Dr Capella recorded in a memorandum to the hospital medical superintendent that 'although there is a great deal of evidence of genetic pre-disposition to this illness xxxx there seems evidence that there is other superadded psychopathology. I have recorded this in the clinical file as adolescent adjustment problem with difficulties in her relationships with both parents, especially with her father.' [Note: 'xxxx' takes the place of some information that was blacked out in the reports.]

He continued in this memo, 'There is a great deal of pathology in this family and the interactions and relationships seem very pathologic. Margaret's mother had xxxx for many years, and it seems strange that she has now improved from her xxxx while Margaret is the depressed and at times hypomanic patient. Xxxx in her life time and Mr Oliver's strong feelings regarding this matter seemed to have largely contributed to his attitude towards Margaret's present illness.'

When the social worker tried to discuss my earlier hospital admissions, my father said that he had taken an interest in psychiatry for many years and 'had diagnosed Margaret before she even saw a psychiatrist.' (FOI Notes)

The whole interview brought out nothing but recriminations, arguments, and my tears.

Dr Capella stated in his report, 'Mrs Oliver appeared to be very much dominated by her husband. Frequently through this interview he told her to be quiet or talked her down. He regularly silenced her by merely glancing at her and frequently they seemed to communicate in this manner by glancing most pointedly at each other.' (FOI Notes)

Dr Capella stated in his report that this interview was to try and have my family look at the problems within it, especially the interactional problems and to try to help us come to an agreement on some acceptable plan for my future.

He further reported, 'During the interview it became very obvious that any interaction between this family very quickly became hostile and an aggressive one.

'Mr Oliver sat throughout the interview with his back turned towards Margaret and directed his questions and statements, even though they were referred to Margaret, towards me.

'Frequent hostile interchanges occurred between Margaret and her mother, and between Margaret and her father, and any attempted discussion between them very quickly degenerated into hostile confrontations, accusations, and tears from Margaret.

'Mr Oliver denied there was anything unusual in the family and refused to accept that the sort of interaction that was being demonstrated at this interview might have anything to do with Margaret's illness and behaviour disturbance.

'He stated that many psychiatrists had seen Margaret, but none of them had ever suggested that this may have been a family problem, and he openly wondered if I was some sort of genius to have identified this.

'He certainly indicated that it in no way agreed with the way he saw Margaret's illness and that he was quite unwilling to accept that the pathologic family interactions had any part to play. He sees the interactions which occur to be solely a result of a pathology in Margaret.' (FOI Notes)

I, of course, was unaware of the wording of this memorandum, or of the significance of the blacked out parts. I only saw these notes twenty-three years later as part of the Freedom of Information Act, although these too became cryptic clues to my genetic heritage.

My understanding from this interview and my earlier discussions with Dr Capella was: 'There's nothing wrong with you; you just don't get on with your parents.'

When I asked my mother when I would be going home, she said, 'When you're better!'

So this was the situation as I saw it. The doctor said I was okay; he was to be taken off my case over my head; and I would be going home when I was better.

Dr Capella felt that, if I went home with my parents, it would only create further difficulties. We could never achieve a productive family life because there was so much hostility between the members of the family. He suggested that I be placed within a church hostel with regular visits and contact from the family.

Maybe I didn't like the alternative, so, in spite of everything, I agreed to go home on a trial basis and look for interim employment for the next five months before returning to my nursing training at the beginning of the following year.

Chapter 5

After seeing Dr Capella on the day I was due to leave, he again confirmed that I was well with no signs at all of manic depression. (FOI Notes)

I rang my father, who came to pick me up. No sooner had he arrived than he started questioning me about the whereabouts of a transistor radio he had given me a year previously. An argument ensued and was witnessed by Dr Capella. (FOI Notes)

Nevertheless, I went home as arranged. This dispute lasted all day, over and over. My father had taken my bankbook from me before I went to hospital and refused to give it back to me. I was seventeen years old, and I had savings and was receiving sickness benefit at the time.

By mid-afternoon, I had had enough of all the arguments and the injustice. At half past three in the afternoon, I slipped away from my parents' gaze, ran to the station, and caught a train back to the hospital.

I told them I had come back early, and spent the night there. Meantime my parents were looking furiously for me. They had called in the police and the whole bit. They hadn't thought of looking for me at the hospital!

No doubt this was all very distressing for my parents, but it was distressing for me too. The next day I caught a train from the hospital and went to see Lang, Heming & Hall, solicitors I had looked up in the phone book. I told them my story and requested that they write a letter so I could get my bankbook back. I then went to see my grandmother, and it was here that the police picked me up on my father's direction.

Dr Capella interviewed me and confirmed that I was perfectly well, in spite of everything. Mr Lang from the solicitor's office had also rung him in relation to my bankbook, which he felt was rightfully mine, but Dr Capella told him that he was 'unable to take any action in this direction and that he did not see it as a medical duty.' (FOI Notes)

I agreed to stay at the hospital until the social worker could find hostel accommodation for me as Dr Capella had previously recommended. (FOI Notes) In the meantime, I overheard a telephone conversation between Dr Capella and my father, who obviously wanted me put in a locked ward.

Although Dr Capella said that I was psychiatrically well and that he did not feel this action would be clinically justified, I did not believe that my father would let it stay like that for long. He had already threatened to take Dr Capella off my case, and not many doctors would stand up to him as Dr Capella had.

This to me was some sort of uncertain death sentence, or life in the loony bin! So I decided that I would leave the hospital without permission, with only the clothes I was wearing, destination unknown. And so I did . . .

I was very scared as I left the hospital grounds, running towards the highway over the railway line. Darkness was approaching, and I could hear dogs barking somewhere in the background.

I half ran and half walked till I could see the railway track, but a six-foot wire fence barred my way. Awkwardly I climbed over it, my heart racing, and crossed the railway track after scanning both ways in case a train was coming.

I could hear the highway traffic nearby, but it meant that I still had a very difficult climb and stumble to the top of the rise. It had looked impossible when I first confronted it, but I kept pushing myself on—I had to get away!

Over and over in my mind, I kept reliving the last interview with Dr Capella and my parents. It seemed inconceivable to me that my future was to be controlled by my parents who were now going to dismiss a doctor who disagreed with them, and presumably leave me to rot in a psychiatric hospital. Well, no thank you!

I was tired, covered in scratches and dirt, and very dishevelled. The highway, and a possible ride away from the area, was only a few feet away now.

I had done it! I had made it to the highway!

That moment of elation was short lived as I then contemplated the prospect of hitching a ride, when I had no real destination, no money, and a very strange reason for needing a ride. Besides which, I had never hitchhiked before.

I began walking along the highway, first wondering if anyone would stop, and then wondering how I would feel if they did stop.

But I was committed to making my 'escape', and the next minute an old battered Holden pulled up beside me. I was very wary of getting in because there were three guys in the car, and they looked pretty rough to me.

However, as they were the only people who had stopped so far, and I needed to get out of the area, I took a chance.

In spite of their appearance, they were not violent or aggressive, and I stayed with them for several days, putting up with their unwanted but persistent attention.

I did not know where I could go, or where destiny would lead me, but I was definitely not going back to the certain misery I'd left behind at the hospital, and I could not stay where I was.

Later that week, just before dusk, I was obligingly dropped off farther along the same highway where I had first met them.

Time passed. Daylight was fading quickly. Traffic lights were blurring as cars passed me in both directions. I was beginning to despair that no one would stop for me, and I was starting to feel hungry, tired, all alone, and very apprehensive.

Then I noticed a light flashing about ten metres in front of me—yes! For some reason, besides being desperate, I had a good feeling about this lift.

The man and his teenage daughter who picked me up became my guardian angels. They were very kind and took me to their home. They cooked me some fried eggs, which I really appreciated. They listened to my story, and I told them I wanted to find work and start my life over. I stayed there for several weeks, and we even visited my parents so they would know I was all right.

My parents could not persuade me to stay and did not exert any force to make me do so. We left without giving my new address, and with $20 from my father, towards my upkeep.

During this time, I contemplated my situation. I wanted to leave where I was, but I still had no job although I had applied for one without result. I thought that my parents were being more reasonable as they had let me go when we visited them, and even contributed to my living costs. So, one day when I developed a high fever, I rang them up and they came and picked me up. I hoped they would realize that I had been living with this family without any problems for two months, and that we might be able to reconcile our differences.

However, nothing was further from their minds. I was taken to two doctors, neither of whom was prepared to regulate me, so my parents instigated my admission themselves and took me down to Wolston Park.

I felt reconciled, though not happy, that my actions on my escape had been necessary for my survival; I had had no other choice.

Once again, I was thrust back into the unreal environment of the psyche hospital, readmitted to Noble House B, and highly medicated.

This made me very angry and resentful towards my parents, as I believed I was being victimized and hospitalized unnecessarily. This was the very reason I had made my escape bid in the first place.

Claiming I had left the hospital because I was 'high' and uncontrollable, my parents saw this as the only place for me.

Apparently, I would be there for the duration.

Chapter 6

Always it was at the back of my mind that I needed to get right away from the hospital and from my parents, who seemed to see no other solution than to keep me there, even when the situation did not support it.

I renewed my friendship with Tom, who had been a patient in this ward when I'd first been there. Tom could be described as a likeable rogue, who by his own admission had a string of break-and-enter convictions, a cheeky sense of humour, and a love of freedom that matched my own.

My parents had met Tom, and they responded with a big thumbs-down as might be expected. However, they had no control over our developing friendship, and there was nothing they could do about it.

It did not take very long for us to begin formulating a plan to get out of there, once and for all!

I knew full well that leaving without a destination was full of pitfalls, and the likelihood of ending up in an even worse situation was ever present. Going alone was also a very dicey option.

So this time, Tom, myself and another freedom lover, Roley, planned our escape. Tom had a brother who lived in Parramatta, and if we could make it there, we would be able to make a fresh start. Tom was discharged from the hospital on the same day that we put our plan into action.

We left during daylight hours, with one suitcase for all of us, and very little money. This time we walked to the nearest train station and caught a train to the interstate railway station.

As we had money for only one ticket, which I carried, Tom and Roley entered the train with only platform tickets. Halfway down to our destination of Sydney, we were found out, and two of us were about to be evicted at the next stop. However, kind fellow passengers, seeing our plight, paid for the other tickets. We felt God was with us!

We arrived at Central Station, Sydney, knowing that the more distance we could put between us and the hospital, the better. It was hot, and we were tired, hungry, and thirsty—but very optimistic!

As we could not find the phone number for Tom's brother in the Sydney directory, we needed money to get to Parramatta and try from there. We agreed that I would be the best person to try and raise some money.

So, I walked around telling people that I had lost my luggage, and could they give me any money so I could go 'home'?

One lady gave me a dollar. I walked around for about ten more minutes, and being unsuccessful in raising any more money, I walked back to my friends.

This same lady had been watching me, and then reported me to the nearby police station, saying that I had taken money from her under false pretences, as we had a suitcase. And it all came under the illegal activity of—you guessed it—'begging for alms'!

So there it was. We were interviewed separately in different rooms. Tom and Roley were released, and I was sent to a shelter in Glebe.

There were about twenty teenage girls there. We wore green tunics and ill-fitting shoes. We spent most of the time sitting around a long plank table in the middle of a small, stuffy room, listening to the radio.

With the girls talking together all the time, the noise in this room was almost unbearable. As a punishment for too much noise, we lost the privilege of listening to the radio (bliss!).

We also had a work schedule, which involved scrubbing the brick floors that were a feature of this shelter. Some of the girls were also allowed to go out in the evening, but I was not one of them.

One week later, they found out who I was and where I was from. My father agreed to pay for my flight back. So it was a police escort for me to Sydney Airport, and on arrival at the Brisbane Domestic Terminal, another police courtesy trip to Wolston Park.

I knew that my parents would be furious, and so they were. This is revealed in a memorandum from Dr Capella to the hospital superintendent: 'Mr Oliver has again contacted the hospital in a most aggressive manner and is demanding Margaret's detention in a closed ward.' (FOI Notes)

He continued: 'I feel there is no clinical indication for such an action. I have again seen Margaret today and again find no evidence that she is suffering from a psychotic illness. There is no doubt that she is behaviour disordered, and there seems to be no doubt that a great deal of her pathology arises out of the difficult family relationships and interactions.'

Looking back on this time, what is really striking to me, is that Dr Capella was prepared to say what he believed and act upon his beliefs with integrity. Instead of bowing down to pressure and legal threats from my father, Dr Capella arranged for me to work in the hospital canteen, which I did. This consisted of helping to prepare food and performing cleaning duties, for which I was 'paid' $1 per day in goods from the canteen.

So life went on—to a degree. I can only imagine the atmosphere at the family home. My parents would be venting their fury and going over and over events, thinking of ways to take legal action against the hospital for my escape and consequent remainder in an open ward under extra observation.

The fact that I was trusted to work in the canteen would have really irked them. How my brother Bobby, then aged twelve years, was able to survive and achieve in this environment speaks very highly of him.

As for myself, I had no symptoms of manic depression, yet I was still in hospital. My bid for freedom had been very unsuccessful!

Over the next few months, I obtained work in a convalescent home and moved into a church hostel. I remained clinically well and saw my parents on the weekends. I still saw Tom every night. He had hitchhiked back from Sydney, but my dissatisfaction with the whole situation was still there, and when Tom suggested that we go back to Sydney, I agreed.

We caught the same train again, this time able to pay for both our tickets. We got out a station earlier than last time, but—surprise, surprise—the police were waiting for us!

So it was straight out to the Glebe shelter for me, and then a flight back at my father's expense once again.

Tom also came back, but was very disillusioned with his own personal problems, and attempted suicide with an overdose of strong pain-killing tablets. He was hospitalized for a month.

Because I had been missing meals by going out with Tom every night, I was asked to leave the hostel, which made working at the convalescent home impossible. So I moved home.

Remarkably, my parents took an unexpected turn and asked Tom to accompany the family on a holiday to Tin Can Bay after his release from hospital. Father's best mate, Bluey, who had been in the air force with him, often used to travel to Tin Can Bay to go crabbing. He was always very enthusiastic about it, and Father asked if he could find us a cheap place to stay for a few weeks.

As such, the house we stayed in had very few modern amenities. Every morning, Tom, Bobby, and I went to pick up ice for the ice chest. The kitchen was equipped with a very old combustion stove. We all showered at the caravan park across the road, and the sand flies bit at night!

We went swimming at the jetty pool, and I had put on so much weight as result of medication that I needed assistance to climb out of the pool.

I thought it was a generous gesture on my parents' part to ask Tom along, but for whatever reason, the day before the end of our holiday, Tom said he was leaving. My father gave him $5 when he left, and it was another six months before I saw him for the last time.

Chapter 7

It was now two years since my initial diagnosis. Whilst still unconvinced that the medication was necessary, and for a 'real' illness, I was taking my lithium tablets.

I set my sights on teaching myself to touch type using my father's notes from when he had been an instructor in the Royal Australian Air Force. I also attended a three-week course at the Reception Centre, and sat for the qualifying examination to work in the Public Service. I was successful in this, and started work at the Taxation Department. I was then eighteen years of age.

Dr Capella had been seeing me every two months. Life at home seemed more tolerable, and my parents were very pleased when I started my new job.

However, that was soon to change . . .

The catalyst was that I met a new boyfriend. My parents had never approved, for one reason or another, of any boy I had ever met. This was to be no different.

Underneath it all, I was still seeking their approval, and for this reason, I invited Tony to meet them. My father's sarcasm and negativity dominated the meeting. Tony was not working at the time, and I wanted to make a fresh start somewhere far away from my home environment. We wanted to go on a working holiday around Australia.

Once again I felt under attack. My parents resumed their constant criticism, not to mention that they always talked about everything over and over. When I went to bed I could still hear them, and I kept thinking over all the events of my life leading up to that time.

One morning, after my parents delivered a particularly scathing attack on Tony's character and his motives for being with me, I packed up most of my belongings and moved into a flat by myself in New Farm, an inner suburb of Brisbane. I continued working at the Taxation Department for several weeks after this.

By then, Tony had a job with Thiess Brothers in Brisbane, and after he visited his brother in Sydney, he was going to work with Thiess Brothers in North Queensland.

I resigned from my job after working there for five months so I could collect my holiday pay before we left. After all, my father had said to Tony that he would apologise to him when we came back, if we actually did go on a working holiday.

During the week after I resigned, I found out that my parents had somehow managed to freeze my bank account so I could not touch my own money. In the meantime I visited another private doctor, Dr Porter, whom I had seen once before, and had a serum lithium test done. I wanted to prove that I had been taking my tablets.

I arranged an interview with Dr Capella and asked my parents to attend. My father kept insisting I had been sacked, but Dr Capella rang my boss on the spot and was told I had been a good worker and had not been asked to leave.

Both my parents claimed that they liked Tony, but thought our plan was impractical. I reminded them that just the day before my father had described Tony as a 'bludger' and myself as a 'slut'. I then queried how he felt my mother's actions fitted in with this definition.

Dr Capella confirmed in his interview notes that 'there was no evidence of mental illness, and no need for hospitalization.' (FOI Notes) He also told us during the interview that Dr Porter had phoned to confirm that my serum lithium was at an acceptable level.

Dr Capella recorded that during the whole of this interview my parents quarrelled and interjected, my father rattling his car keys to silence my mother when she tried to speak.

My parents didn't want me to leave. Maybe my plan was a wise choice; maybe it wasn't. But I was an adult now, and it was my decision. I agreed to bring Tony to meet Dr Capella the following afternoon at two o'clock.

You might be forgiven for thinking, as I did, that this was a positive result. After the interview, I hurriedly made my way to Tony's flat to give him the happy result and ask him to come and meet Dr Capella the next day. Tony was not home when I got there, so I waited for him. He got home late and I stayed the night—well, part of the night.

A loud banging on the door in the early hours of the morning startled Tony and me awake. It was the police, who had instructions to take me to Wolston Park. They forcibly removed me and took me, protesting, to the hospital, where I was taken to an antiquated closed ward called Female Eight.

On arrival in the ward, I put up the struggle of my life, breaking the male assistant's glasses in the process. He repaid me for this later when I was put in a room. He grabbed me by the hair and slammed my head onto the concrete floor at least twelve times. This was followed by an injection and then complete isolation in a locked room, where I spent the rest of the night stumbling round and round in a daze.

Why had I put up such a struggle? Because I shouldn't have been there! Dr Capella, whom I had seen the previous day, backed up by Dr Porter, had both confirmed I had no signs of mental illness and didn't require hospitalization.

The question I asked myself at the time and on so many other occasions, was, *Why did my parents want me locked up?*

It turned out that my father had made good his threat of contacting the director general of health. In addition, his previous request to the superintendent of the hospital to transfer me to a different doctor's care, as my parents 'had no faith in Dr Capella's methods', was put into place. (Quote from a copy of my mother's letter to the superintendent in my FOI Notes)

Notwithstanding all the evidence to the contrary, I was now a regulated patient again in what could only be described as a little hellhole!

For the enlightenment of those who have never been in such a hovel, let me give you a brief description: Female Eight consisted of about fifteen cell-like rooms with concrete floors. A solid mattress was bolted onto the floor. This was what we slept on, and we were indeed fortunate if we managed to secure a blanket. A small black bucket was provided in case we wanted to go to the toilet. There was a kind of a shutter that could be closed over the window so that there was absolutely no light in the room. The light switch was on the outside, and when the light was not left on all night, we were in total darkness from the moment we entered our room to the moment we were released in the morning at half past six. We then had to scrub the floor of our cells and have a shower—all the girls together.

After that came breakfast, which I can find no words to adequately describe.

Everyone had her duties, and mine at this time consisted of working in the kitchen. This meant I had to mop the floors so that they were clean all day, and wash all the cups, plates, and cutlery that were used during meal times. Another couple of girls wiped the dishes and put them away.

We all wore ward clothes—cotton shifts that never kept us warm. When it was really cold, we were given a windcheater, shrunk to half its size.

After breakfast in the tiny dining room, which was so small you couldn't swing a rat, we were herded out onto the terrace veranda. That may sound very luxurious—terrace veranda—but read on for further details.

The veranda was about four feet wide by forty feet long, and was divided into three long, dark terraces. It was extremely cold in the mornings as the sun could only be found along the top three feet of the veranda.

I can still vividly recall one morning. I was sitting at the bottom level when another patient crept up quietly behind me with a heavy leather pillow from an armchair and belted me nearly unconscious with it.

There was, as well, one permanent resident of the veranda. This unfortunate soul was permanently strapped into a large chair, and I was told she had been transferred to Female Eight after she had bitten a woman in her previous ward who had subsequently died. Rowena was like a big child who had never grown up, but she was very violent when she broke loose. She would bang her head hard against the heavy wooden door to the veranda, and her skull at the front looked as if it was about four inches thick.

If you didn't mind obscene language twenty-four hours a day, physical violence and arguments, and the dispensing of punishments by way of drugs and sheer brutality by the so-called nursing staff, you might have had a chance in Female Eight.

There was only one male in the place, who also supervised the kitchen and assisted the female staff when they could not handle situations that frequently arose.

In later years, they introduced more male nursing staff to Female Eight, and I can assure you that the most this achieved was an increase in brutality and hardships for the patients, of which I was one.

However, I must also mention that there were some good nurses who tried hard to look after the patients and make their stays more pleasant.

Chapter 8

After my traumatic arrival at Female Eight, can you imagine how I was feeling the next morning? I'd been physically abused, drugged, and incarcerated in a locked room. All this after being woken from sleep in a peaceful and safe environment, and forcibly taken to this hospital ward for 'treatment'. I was understandably angry and felt there was absolutely no justice. My new doctor, Dr Samuel, described my presentation after she interviewed me: 'It was almost impossible to get a history at this interview because Margaret's speech is slurred because she has received Melleril [thioridazine].

'When I arrived at the ward she was smelly—had faeces wiped all over her. She was ataxic and drowsy.

'This morning she was reported to have attacked a male nurse—she admitted injuring him and using terrible language—she said she had gone for about five of them (i.e. nursing staff).

'She is, despite her medication, exhibiting pressure of talk, loose association, and disinhibition. I have signed a seclusion order in case this is necessary again.'

In addition to Melleril, I was put on lithium carbonate and other sedative medications if necessary.

As my readers may recall, I was already taking lithium carbonate and had had a satisfactory level recorded only two days before this whole fiasco.

The diagnosis this time was 'manic depressive psychosis in hypomanic state'. (FOI Notes)

I put it to you, the reader: After all that treatment, who wouldn't be? All of this occurred in the space of four hours, including police intervention!

Tony was waiting to visit me the next morning but was told that I was not well enough to see him then. He was advised to make an appointment with my doctor for the following week.

Tony then visited my solicitors, Lang, Heming & Hall, and returned with a letter that requested he be allowed to visit me, 'if that is consistent with our client's state of health.' (FOI Notes) He was again refused a visit.

Three days later, he came in to have an interview with Dr Samuel; he had made this appointment earlier during the week. Here is a transcript of this interview taken from my Freedom of Information notes: 'Interview with Tony, Margaret's boyfriend.

'This 23-year-old boy seems warm and stable. He speaks fairly good English despite the fact that he has been in Australia only 2 years (born in Czechoslovakia but lived in Yugoslavia).

'He feels that Margaret has not changed in the 4 months that he has known her—the change came only when her parents reacted so strongly to Margaret leaving a job which bored her, and proposing that she go to Sydney with him. He feels her reactions are quite understandable in the light of her parents' behaviour.

'He says that they confuse him, too, "First it's all right, then it isn't, then it is and then it isn't."

'He does not regard Margaret as having spent money unreasonably—in any case, "it was her own money which her parents are currently controlling."

Dr Samuel then invited me into the interview room. The following is the transcript of this interview taken from Dr Samuel's notes, released under the Freedom of Information Act:

'Margaret speaks under pressure but is not elated. Is fairly controlled—not very disinhibited.

'Tells her life story with appropriate feeling. Says she want us to try "to straighten out this business once and for all so that her parents can't push me in here every time they feel like it." Shows a great deal of insight into her own and some of her parents' feelings.'

Several more days progressed, during which time I was trying to regain my dignity and behave a little more calmly. I was still trying to prove that I was 'all right', and under the circumstances plus strong medication, it was no easy task, but I persevered.

Ten days after this admission, I was given a day's parole on the hospital grounds. In four days' time, I was to be transferred to an open ward.

My parents saw Dr Samuel the day before my scheduled transfer and were given permission to take me to the canteen for half an hour.

Dr Samuel recorded in her clinical notes: 'Just as they were all leaving, there were some angry remarks from Margaret about the selection of clothes they had brought for her preparatory to her going to an open ward.'

I thought it was very interesting on reading these notes years later, that she went on to add, 'I can only hope that this or a further argument does not flare while they are together, resulting in some impulsive action—e.g. absconding on Margaret's part.'

When Dr Capella was transferred off my case, the last paragraph in his memorandum to the hospital superintendent, stated: 'Though I understand Mr Oliver's concern for his daughter and especially for the risk to her when she leaves in the company of various young men, and though I understand his great concern about this, I still feel that much of Margaret's behaviour is reactive and provocative and punishing of her family, especially of her father.

'It is unfortunate that I have never been able to have Mr Oliver see this as a possible explanation of her behaviour.' (FOI Notes)

Dr Samuel seems to have given credence to this effect of family interaction and reaction after only one interview.

However, the door was also closed to any more investigation into the situation that had precipitated my leaving home in the first place. It was also closed to any possibility that this may have been seen as a reasonable response to a hostile, unjust environment, rather than as a symptom of manic depression.

The following day, on returning to an open ward, I adopted the attitude that, 'Even if you can keep me here, you can't stop me working.'

Remarkably, straight off, on that first day, after seeing a social worker, I was given permission to leave the hospital to seek employment.

My first job was with a research-advertising firm that promoted the sale of publications of various kinds. This translated as selling encyclopaedia's door to door. In actual fact, I was dropped off at a certain location and picked up at the end of the day. This meant that oftentimes it was evening before I arrived back at the hospital. Thus, permission was withdrawn for me to continue this job.

I was not happy with that decision, plus I knew Tony would be leaving soon to transfer up north for his work. I therefore left the hospital early the next morning and caught a taxi to visit Tony before he left.

He was not at home, and as I had been relying on him to pay my not-inconsiderable cab fare, I was taken by the cab driver to the nearest police station. They rang my father, who agreed to pay for that fare plus one back to the hospital.

I wonder if you can guess which ward I went to?

You guessed it—back to Female Eight!

During this period, as always, I continually actively disputed my need for lithium or any other sedative medications.

I had observed that, if a patient came to hospital and was agitated and abusive because of the situation or the way he or she had been brought in, they would pump the patient full of medication till he or she could hardly think anymore, then start to reduce it, and say the patient was getting better. It had certainly been my experience.

As I lay on my 'mattress' on the floor of my 'cell', contemplating my whole situation, my eyes focused on the big, wooden door, and ultimately on the keyhole. It was during this stay that I came to the conclusion that, if I ever wrote a book about these experiences, I would call it, *From the Inside of the Keyhole*.

After a month of 'refresh and contemplation', I was transferred back to the open ward and resumed looking for work. Within a week I had a full-time job as a clerk at Brisco Butler Automotive Services. I attended work from the hospital for six weeks before returning home to go to work from there.

It seems amazing, as I look back, that one minute I was being detained in a closed ward, and one week later I was well and able to work.

I continued writing to Tony and saw him occasionally when he was down in Brisbane. After two months, Dr Samuel allowed me to stop taking the Melleril, which had made me feel sleepy in this sedentary occupation. I stayed at this job for nine months, and never had any problems at all. The main problem for me was that nothing had happened that convinced me I had any illness or any need for medication.

I was now nineteen years of age, and it had been three years since my diagnosis of manic-depressive psychosis. As far as I could see, everything I had done and felt had been for a reason. My very worst experiences had been caused by being locked up and drugged up for no just cause, together with being angry and humiliated, yet trying to be seen as 'normal'.

I didn't want to just show that I could do a job. I wanted to start off somewhere fresh where nobody knew any of this history. I wanted to prove that I could live and work successfully without medication and hospitals. However, neither my doctor nor family was interested in this.

So, after scanning the *Courier Mail*, over the phone, I applied for and was accepted to work as a live-in nanny again. This time it was for a father whose wife had left him, but after three weeks, he told me he could not afford to keep the children and was putting them into a home. He gave me $40 pay for the week, and I left.

CHAPTER 9

Predictably, after this failed attempt at freedom and my 'cold turkey' withdrawal from lithium, I found myself returned to hospital, only this time I was placed in the maximum-security ward, Osler House. I will describe this pleasant abode for you on a later visit.

I found it interesting to read a comment in the doctor's clinical notes at this time: 'Parents are a bit difficult. Phoning in every day. Her father is remarkably obsessive, comes in with a graph he had made of all her past mood swings etc.

'He is always arguing about her therapy. In particular, he is upset because she won't take lithium. He seems to think it would affect a permanent cure.

'Apparently he controls her every movement at home. This no doubt leads to her running away from home.'

Feeling doped up on a daily basis was nothing to look forward to either, plus suffering the side effects of various drugs, including being unable to void until I took another drug to counteract that. So this pattern continued for the next few years. It seems, if nothing else, I had inherited the same determination my father exhibited.

In 1974, I returned to nursing and was doing my first year of training to become a registered nurse at the Princess Alexandra Hospital, Brisbane. Initially, my way of dealing with my psychiatric background was to completely ignore it. Indeed, I never mentioned it to anyone.

However, live-in nurses form a close community, and after several months I confided my situation to my closest friend, Vivian. Listening to her life experiences and going out with her convinced me that the freedoms I wanted were no different to hers. So once again I felt encouraged to question my need for medication.

When I first started my training, I was still taking Melleril in addition to lithium. After six months, my doctor still would not let me cease the Melleril. This made it very difficult to stay alert whilst sitting through classroom lectures, which were interspersed with ward work. I had to really concentrate to copy my notes, and at one stage actually closed my eyes whilst the head tutor was looking at me. She took me aside after the lecture, and told me to 'either get off the drugs or get out'.

So I went to a medical practitioner, Dr Mc Nab, and asked him to give me a referral to a private psychiatrist. He referred me to Dr Kaal who told me he could make no conclusions on my story alone without my previous medical reports.

In the meantime, I returned to Dr McNab and told him I wanted to try being off all my medication. He agreed to monitor my progress if I came and saw him on a regular basis.

But the withdrawal was not gradual enough, and after a period of several months, I began to feel disoriented and unhappy about myself. In addition, I had accidentally burnt my hand on the steamer we used for keeping patients' food warm.

So, I went home with Leroy, my boyfriend for a year, to talk about things.

However, I met with a very hostile and sarcastic reception. My parents did not believe I had stopped my medication under a doctor's care, and were not interested in finding out either. They physically stopped me from touching the telephone to ring Dr McNab for verification of this, and instead rang the police to take me to hospital.

Leroy stood there dumbfounded when four or five police officers and I scuffled as they tried to get me in their car. After I received one heavy hit to my face, I lay half on the grass and half in the gutter. Then I was 'helped' into the car and taken to Osler House. Here I was stripped of my watch and rings, given an injection, and left in a locked room. I was so angry! For several weeks, I once again contemplated my present and my future—'from the inside of the keyhole'.

When I was finally discharged, having had plenty of time to consider every angle, I was fed up with the whole deal. I was either persecuted as being 'high' every time I was beginning to recover from the previous episode and take an interest in life, or I was given this murderous treatment when I was willing to admit I needed help.

I wondered what the point of it all was, and I was quite calm and resolute when I approached the railing on our front veranda and considered the impact my weight would make on the pebbled concrete surface fifteen foot down.

With my not-inconsiderable weight, I figured that should do it. Finito!

I went back inside where I had been watching a movie on TV, and then, finally, made up my mind to do it.

I returned to the veranda and leaned on the railing. I swung gently back and forth, and then overbalanced myself so I landed head first on the concrete below.

But then I sat up, and after six stitches on the crown of my head later, at the local hospital, I was back home.

Even though I requested their silence, I still find it ironic that my parents never made any mention to a psychiatrist of my attempt to take my life.

Chapter 10

So, what happens next? What happens after you've seriously analysed your life and found it to have been a cycle of constant defeat? What happens after you've decided there's no point to it all and you've been considering how you could end the vicious cycle? What happens when you carry out a plan you think will work, and nothing happens?

As I had already rejected every other method I could think of, and had survived my last actions without sustaining serious injury or possible paralysis, it was time for me to admit that there was no 'easy' way out.

The comforting fantasy that I would be removed from this testing was gone. I would have to continue living through my life, day by day, with no escape. I would have to continue 'fighting the fight' against worsening odds that I had created for myself, to establish that I could function as a normal person. There was no more time for 'pity parties' about the way my life had deviated from my previous positive anticipation.

Confronting this new reality meant that I also had to accept responsibility for myself, and for those decisions of my own that I could rationalize away, but that had certainly worked against my cause.

When I looked back many years later at the notes written by Dr Capella, I could see how accurate his perception had been when he noted that 'I still feel that much of Margaret's behaviour is reactive and provocative and punishing of her family, especially of her father.'

For, indeed, there was a lot of anger flashing around and within the souls of our 'dysfunctional family'. And most of it was based on the assumption or belief of 'betrayal'—betrayal of trust, betrayal of love, and protective and defensive feelings towards those who had suffered because of this, and feelings of guilt. And it was all caused by love—love in a family that had been nurtured and grown in an atmosphere of warmth, pride in achievement, dependability, safety, and security.

Till that fateful night when I called out I was going for a glass of water . . .

Prior to that event, life in the Oliver household had been happy, with many fun times immortalized in the memories of my brother, Bobby, and me. Happy scenes from my childhood flash before me as I write these pages: The smell of freshly-cut grass as I helped my father rake it into piles whilst my mother tended her vegetable garden, over which she had strung rows of sparkling milk bottle tops to discourage the birds from feasting on her crops. I remember watching the rain streaming down the windows from my playroom where I sat on a cupboard bench, loving my attempts at knitting as my mother had shown me. Then there was the wonder of Christmas morning when I found a beautiful walking bride doll waiting for me—a doll that I still treasure today, who sits in the spare bedroom dressed in pretty summer clothes, and alternatively in warm winter ones. The arrival of my brother, Bobby, a week before my fifth birthday was a happy event. We all went up to the country in our FJ Holden, my brother very cosy in a wooden fruit carton for the trip, to show him to our grandparents and our aunty, uncle, and cousins.

Just two years later, my mother, brother and I were on a flight to Brisbane to be met by our father. Our father was in the Royal Australian Air Force, and had been transferred to the base at Amberley, just outside Ipswich. He was happy about this because his mother, who was now a widow, lived in Brisbane, and we would be living just half an hour's drive away. My mother regretted leaving her friends and family behind to move to 'this hot, dusty hole', which was her description of Ipswich.

But, nevertheless, she made new friends, and several years later, both of her sisters moved up from Victoria. One settled with her husband in Cleveland, and the other, who had been widowed early, had remarried to an Ipswich man and lived just a few suburbs away from us.

A typical Saturday morning would see my father up first, putting on some Scottish music, for he was very proud of his Scottish heritage.

I started learning to play the piano when I was nine years of age, and my parents used to proudly watch me perform at the local eisteddfod.

It was during this time, that my brother became involved in a startling event, which I am sure he remembers even more vividly than I do. I was sitting at the dining room table tracing a map for my geography homework. Suddenly, there was a loud, thundering explosion and the air in the room shuddered blue and yellow.

Behind our house was a large power substation. My mother tore frantically downstairs because she had last seen my brother and his playmate, who lived next door, sitting near the high wire dividing fence.

Happily, both children were safe and unharmed, but they had actually caused the explosion. A choko vine grew along the back fence in our yard, and Bobby and Ayleen had been throwing pieces of the dead vine through the fence. Somehow, one of these pieces earthed a transformer, which in turn caused the massive explosion and blacked out two-thirds of Ipswich! (Incidentally, my brother grew up to become an electrician!)

Christmas holidays were great, because our mother always organized a place for us to stay down at the Gold Coast. We used to have fun swimming, making sand castles and tunnels, and going for walks along the beach collecting shells and stones.

Life was good, and neither Bobby nor myself could anticipate how everything would change when he was in grade three in primary school and I was doing very well in my second year at high school.

It became clear to me during the tormented years that followed that, in spite of all the setbacks, my father still believed in me and my ability to achieve.

My mother, on the other hand, felt that I should not even try to work again, as it would only end up in failure; indeed, she told her friends that I would never be well enough to leave home and manage my own life. But, in spite of her always anxious negativity, I did keep on trying and I did achieve—but not immediately.

Chapter 11

The next two years were like a roller-coaster ride, with few high points and many low points.

When I returned to work at the Princess Alexandra Hospital, I was still on medication, and in spite of this—or because of this—I was unable to sleep at night. This caused me to become increasingly anxious, so I left this position. I was then twenty one years of age.

The main method of treatment I received was the administration of drugs and lithium carbonate. The predominant theory was that 'more' was better than 'less'.

It was all a very tight tapestry—me pulling to be free; my parents wanting to restrain my freedom by unrelenting restrictions and threats to report doctors to higher authorities; and doctors trying to find a balanced treatment that fit within the constraints imposed by my parents.

I was admitted to hospital three times over the next three years based on statements made to the police by my father or my mother. The action of the police was based solely on my parents' say-so, without any further justification needed. I had no chance to repudiate their claims and charges, despite the fact that I was legally an adult.

A confrontation with police who had an order to detain me and take me to a psyche hospital certainly went a long way to ensure that I was not 'cool, calm, collected, and rational' when I arrived at the hospital—such treatment would cause reactive behaviour in anyone.

It amuses me to reflect on my FOI notes, which say on such occasions that I was 'over-talkative with flight of ideas' or 'mildly hypomanic with slight euphoria'. I think such confrontations guarantee a response that might be considered 'abnormal'.

One very memorable event concerned a visit to my grandmother. My brother had started calling her Pi Pi when we first moved to Queensland when he was just two years of age. From then on, this was the affectionate name the whole family used for her.

When we first moved up, we lived with Pi Pi, and she used to take me to school in the bus each morning. In the afternoons, she would return to take me home in the bus. I used to cry every morning before I went to school—it all seemed very different to me from my school in Melbourne. As well, they had a different style of writing in Queensland—cursive, running writing—and I had only learnt script. Every afternoon, I practised the new style from a copybook.

After we moved to Ipswich, we used to visit Pi Pi once a week on the weekend. My father would do odd jobs for her and mow the lawn. We all helped rake up and usually stayed for tea.

My grandmother taught me how to cook a type of pancake called pikelets and how to sew using her Singer treadle sewing machine. I always felt close to my grandmother, and I don't remember her ever having an unkind word for me.

Even when I first went into hospital at sixteen, she only visited once, but I remember her saying to my father, 'She shouldn't be in a place like this.'

Many years later, after she developed diabetes and began to hear noises at night that scared her, she moved into a nursing home near us. This was not her decision, but was considered the most practical by my parents. However, in many ways she flourished—tending her garden, making new friends, and staying there a further eighteen years till she passed away peacefully in her sleep, aged ninety-eight years.

With all that had been happening in my own life, I had not seen her so often, and it was not surprising that when I had the opportunity, I went to visit her. She seemed to be the only person who still believed in me and loved me.

I was living in Mogill and working as a real estate agent at the quickly developing suburb of Bellbowrie. A train and a bus saw me delivered to her doorstep.

When I visited her, she was very pleased to see me. I asked her if I could wear her ruby engagement ring for a day and bring it back the next day. I just wanted to feel special in some way. My grandmother always wore this ring, but she trusted me and lent it to me. The next day, I went back and returned the ring as we had agreed.

Just as I was leaving, one of the nursing staff came up to me and told me I was not allowed to see my grandmother. A few minutes later, the police arrived.

My father had found out that I had visited my grandmother the day before, and told the police I had stolen her ring. My grandmother never said that had happened, and she was wearing it when the police arrived.

Nevertheless, I was carted off to the local police station, told to write a confession, which I refused to do, and spent the night in a holding cell.

Although a charge was drawn up against me, it was dismissed on the same day, because there was no evidence brought up by the police prosecutor to support it. As it was, all the evidence was to the contrary. But was that going to be the end of it? It seemed not. My father made application for my admission to hospital.

After this complete humiliation, a sleepless night in a prison cell, a court appearance, combined with my anger and frustration, I had to then undergo a consultation with a local general practitioner, Dr Cooper, who described me as 'facile, glib, euphoric, pressure of talk and speech, with flight of ideas, grandiose ideas.' He concurred with Section 7(b) of the Mental Health Act, 1974, that it was necessary in the interests of the patient's health and safety or for the protection of others that the patient be so detained for the following reason: 'Patient is unable to care for herself in the community or at home at present.' (FOI Notes)

So there it was. I was again looking at hospital admission!

Six weeks later, when I was being regulated for what was intended to be a twelve-month period, the doctor who had admitted me prepared a review that I only saw many years later in my FOI notes. This showed his assessment of my mental state on the day of admission as, 'very mildly hypomanic', which was quite a contrast to Dr Cooper's statement. The review also noted that for the first three days of my admission I was AWOL (absent without leave). (FOI Notes)

I found the whole episode to be such a fiasco that after being admitted to an open ward and granted permission to go to the canteen, I simply walked out.

On being returned three days later by the police, I was put on Category C in the open ward, meaning I was confined to the ward in my pyjamas. I was on my way out again through the window, wearing a ward dress I had found in a storeroom when I was apprehended and transferred to maximum security, Osler House.

Maybe I asked for that, but to my way of thinking, I should never have been in the hospital at all, let alone going through the process of regulation.

There was a lot of controversy about the so-called theft charges. I was amused to read the letter sent by the deputy medical superintendent, Dr Madison, to the district inspector, Ipswich police station.

Here is the transcript:

Dear Sir,

Re: Margaret Oliver

On 16th June, 1976, I interviewed a person who claimed to be Detective Senior Constable Francis of your C.I.B., who informed me that a charge of stealing was pending against the above-named since 11th June, 1976, and requested that I notify him when she was ready to be discharged from this Hospital, she having been admitted here on the 12th June 1976. He said that he wished to interview the patient after her discharge, with a view to dropping the charge against her.

I now have to hand a letter from the Clerk of the Court at Ipswich, dated 26th July 1976, in which he says that the above-named appeared in court on 10th June 1976 on the same charge, that no evidence was offered by the Police Prosecutor, and that this charge was struck out.

If this letter is true, then the information supplied to me by Detective Senior Constable Francis caused me a great deal of unnecessary work and inconvenience. Under paragraph (1) subsection (1) of Section 34 of the Mental Health Act, 1974, a person in the position represented to me by your Detective Senior Constable has to be treated as a 'restricted patient' under Section 50 of the Mental Health Act, which involves a great deal of record keeping on our part; and, in addition, the psychiatrist in charge of the treatment of the patient is required to submit a lengthy report on the patient's condition, on her fitness to plead, etc., to our Director. It also causes a great deal of difficulty in treating the patient, as once they come under that Section of the Mental Health Act, their future management is governed by Orders of the Governor-in-Council.

This apparent misinformation from one of your officers will make me very cautious about accepting their verbal statements in the future, unless some reasonable explanation of this incident reaches me.

Yours sincerely,

Dr V. L. Madison
Deputy Medical Superintendent

No further correspondence was received from the district inspector. (FOI Notes)

I had always been highly critical of the fact that my 'treatment' was conducted in this large, archaic hospital, which had originally been established in 1865 as the Woogaroo Lunatic Asylum. Since then it had expanded and undergone several name changes, with Wolston Park Psychiatric Hospital being the designated name when I was there.

I was told the reason I was sent to this free public hospital was because of the high cost of private treatment. After my last discharge, three months before this episode, I had taken out private health insurance.

Just three weeks prior to this admission, I had placed myself under the care of Dr Plank, a private psychiatrist who specialized in the diagnosis and treatment of manic depression.

In the middle of August, my father requested and was granted twenty-eight days' leave for me, and Dr Plank had this extended a further six months. He then went to Melbourne to practise, and I transferred to Dr O'Brien, who recommended my discharge following this long leave.

It was quite enlightening and at times traumatic to read the background information behind my treatment. I have quoted from it quite heavily in this chapter to convey to you, the reader, the intensity with which my admissions were sought, and the disrespect I developed for the circumstances of my admissions and the conditions of my treatment.

Chapter 12

And still, over all this period, no one ever talked to me about what may have caused this illness. The only positive information I had about manic depression came from the book my father lent me, *Moodswing* by Dr Ronald Fieve, which outlined the lives of some famous people reputed to have made positive achievements in spite of having this condition.

This book also stated that, although the illness was not caused by a deficiency of lithium, the correct therapeutic level of lithium would correct a chemical imbalance of the brain, which he cited as the reason for mood disturbance. I wondered how they managed to ascertain the correct level, if this was indeed the case.

In spite of my general reluctance to admit that I had an illness, I was learning some important things as I went along. I knew it was no good at all if I couldn't sleep, and my home environment, with repeated conversations and recriminations at times, didn't help. Hospitalization, hostility on my part, and an overload of drugs were certainly reflected in a very poor sleep pattern also.

It became logical and obvious to me that the only way to gain the upper hand with this illness was that I had to be the one in control. I had to be the one to realize if things weren't right and to set them straight. But at this time, I did not know how to accomplish this.

One instance stands out clearly upon reflection. One particular week, I had been unable to sleep, and my boyfriend at the time was very supportive of me and took me to his doctor. I explained my situation, and he gave me a prescription for chloral hydrate. So I went home and got ready for bed. I was then going to take this medication and hopefully get a good night's sleep.

But no—my mother seemed to have her own agenda. She was in and out of my room, and would not give me any peace or a chance to take the medication.

She began taunting me and arguing with me, and ran out of the house into the street, screaming. So, the police were called, and I was once again taken to hospital. The following week, my mother was admitted to the same hospital for two weeks herself.

You can imagine my frustration. I knew I needed sleep. I had tried to remedy my sleep problem in a responsible way, and instead I was once again taken forcefully to hospital.

As I was considered a bad flight risk (and admittedly I was), I was sent straight to the maximum-security ward, Osler House, a place with which I had become very familiar.

Once again I had the opportunity to consider my situation 'from the inside of the keyhole', and to consider why it was that my mother seemed to completely overreact to every situation. Her logic didn't make sense to me. She always seemed to come from some completely different tangent, which ensured that the lack of trust between us continued to grow. However, I could understand her frustration also.

But for now, to leave those contemplations aside, let me introduce you to the well-hidden humour that existed in the maximum security and closed wards such as Osler House and Female Eight. In these wards, it was the 'key' that dominated activities. The 'key' decided whether you went into the yard or came inside to the loo, or whether the 'cell' door was unlocked and relocked, leaving you to enjoy a 'peaceful' rest under lock and key, until half past six in the morning. *Peace*—now there's a word that signifies a joke, for all night long, you would hear inmates thumping on the walls of their cells, and people crying out to be heard.

The reason for this was anger combined with helplessness, or merely the want of a glass of water, or perhaps a request for the time, or, for newcomers, an assuaging of the fear they must feel and the need for reassurance.

After exhausting my lungs one night for a glass of water and not receiving one, I began scraping my metal bed around my cell and making a terrific noise. So intent was I to make noise that the bed started falling apart and I systematically pushed it, piece by piece, outside the building, through the bars of my cell window, which of course left me with no bed at all.

I never did get my glass of water; when the nursing staff finally realized what I had done, I was given some 'T.L.C.' and an injection, which I didn't enjoy at all.

Injections were almost a way of life—nobody liked them, but if someone else received one, a spirit of gaiety was common amongst the other inmates.

The residents of the maximum-security ward were predominantly the rebellious, the uncontrollable, the unreachable, the sensitive, and the brilliant, with one thing in common—they all wished desperately to be free.

Thus the main positive attitude emanating from the maximum-security ward was hope—hope to be freed and to experience the joy of leaving that lifestyle behind, as you vowed never to return—a positive and determined statement. And, my, didn't the sun shine so brightly on the outside of that infernal enclosing wire fence.

Previously, I mentioned the 'key'. This, of course, referred to the nursing staff and the power they had over the residents' movements. The doctors were, in fact, 'the door'. They alone could discharge a patient, even if only to the more-favoured open ward. He or she also ordered the specific medication for each patient, so specific that many patients suffered a drug-induced haze that kept them barely able to think straight. I know, for I have been there, and I have known the despair, as no doubt many of my readers have also.

I shall relate one further incident that occurred during my stay in maximum security. I see the humour in it as I look back, but I did not see any humour at the time. One day, the key to the kitchen cupboard, which housed the table knives, went missing. All the patients were searched in their individual rooms, but nothing was found. That night, on change of shift, I heard a sound under my door. The patient in the room next to mine—one of the 'favoured' ones allowed to stay up—had pushed the missing key under my door, and then reported that she thought I was the one who had taken it.

Two nurses then came into my room and found the key where it had been slid through. For this, although completely innocent, I received one week locked in my room. My meals were delivered with plastic cutlery, and all I had for company was my usual comfort bucket.

Chapter 13

My desire to be free, happy, and successful seemed a very elusive goal.

As I flip through my Freedom of Information notes and see the plethora of drugs, the frequency of seclusion, the anger I felt, and the hostility I displayed at times, it seems almost unbelievable that from any combination of these, a rational, peaceful individual could ever emerge.

It seemed equally unlikely that I could still have retained hope and belief in myself, but I did.

Another thing I had learnt was that, with only desperation to guide me, I could walk out into the night with nothing, hitch a ride, and survive. Maybe I had a guardian angel who always travelled with me, although on one occasion when a companion and I were thumbing a ride at night, a car pulled up containing the police officers who were actually searching for us—so back we went!

Mental health tribunals were also another avenue that was available to patients to plead their cases, as it were, in an attempt to regain their freedom.

Being in an open ward was definitely preferable to being in a closed ward, and there was an occasion when I was convinced I was going to be transferred back to a closed ward. So, to use a colloquial expression, I 'took off'. I guess I was a lot of trouble for the nurses in charge, but as I watched a search begin, I made my way, under cover of the bush, to a railway station where I later boarded a train.

The reason I relate this story is that I had already had a hearing with the revue tribunal coming up, and although I was 'out' of hospital, I still made my way to where the tribunal was to be held. I wanted to put forward my viewpoint on my hospitalization—I was still hoping to be legitimately set free. I wanted to establish that everything I did was not done because I had a mental illness. However, this did not work in my favour, and I was reinstalled to my previous abode.

I must admit, though, things were always a little bit more complex. Here is an example: I had met Adam when I was on one of my escapades from the hospital. When he learned where I was from, Adam had rung the police, and I had been returned to the maximum-security ward. Of course, I wasn't happy about this turn of events, but then Adam started visiting me.

After I was transferred to an open ward, Adam became much more adventurous, and I would sneak out at night to meet him, and after an evening out, he would return me to the ward, which I re-entered via the same window through which I had left. My 'dummy' made up of blankets and pillow would wait up for me. It was surprising how well that worked. Even when the substitute was finally discovered, when I came in, I said I'd just been sitting down at the bowling green on the hospital grounds, and nothing ever came of that.

Eventually, I was discharged into my parents' care, and Adam continued to visit me at home and take me out every two or three weeks. We talked on the phone and sent taped letters to each other. Adam was the type of guy who made me feel special, and that was a happy time in my life.

Although he was fully aware of my situation, Adam accepted me and wanted to marry me. He said he would understand if I was a little 'crazy' sometimes, and that life with me would never be boring. He said that with laughter in his voice.

My dad tried to talk him out of this, but Adam was quite resolute and would not be deterred. My parents met with his mother, and the announcement was placed in the paper. It was quite a magical time.

However, as time went on, I began to have my own doubts. This was mainly centred on the fact that Adam worked only a series of casual jobs owing to a back problem caused by years of heavy demolition work, and he didn't pay his bills. I didn't find this reassuring for the long term, and although it wasn't easy, I broke it off.

A short while later, I was working at a private hospital in Ipswich and living in nurses' accommodation across the road from the hospital. After nearly three months, Adam rang and wanted to go out with me, one of his mates, and a nursing friend of mine. So, it was agreed, for old times' sake.

We went down to Brisbane by train, and as the evening progressed, Adam and my girlfriend, Chris, were together, and Ken and I were together. We'd been to a nightclub and a piano bar, and it was too late to go back to Ipswich, so I stayed with Ken, and Chris stayed with Adam, by mutual agreement.

It seemed, however, that Adam wasn't really happy with this arrangement. The next day, Ken and I were walking down one of the main streets of Brisbane. The next minute, Adam arrived in a fever with two policemen in tow. Adam was adamant that I was sick, and he had a court order for me to go to hospital.

The scene was really quite comical. Adam was shouting; a little old lady was tapping him on the shoulder with an umbrella telling him to calm down; Ken was goading Adam till Adam punched him; and Ken punched him back a better one.

Adam insisted on going with me and the police to the outpatient department of a nearby public hospital, the Royal Brisbane Hospital, where coincidentally I had first been diagnosed. Adam sat in the front, and the cop driving said, 'I don't want him in here with me!'

I exclaimed, 'I don't want him in the back with me either!'

Can you see my situation now?

After all that, I had to go and represent myself as being calm, cool, collected, sane, and in charge of my actions, and always with my previous history to contend with. Had I really done anything to justify a court order, possible hospitalization, and being apprehended in one of Brisbane's main streets, and carted away in a police vehicle?

Fortunately, for once, I managed to remain calm. One policeman dropped the other policeman and me off at outpatients, and the other took Adam home. The police officer who accompanied me was sympathetic to my situation and spoke up for me. I told the doctor I was taking lithium, which I was, and they took a blood test to substantiate this.

In the meantime, I also received a supply of tablets from them. Miraculously, they said I was free to go—this was such a feeling of achievement for me, and the first time it had ever happened!

The proverbial Blind Freddy could see that Adam had been in touch with my parents to even know about court orders and the procedure, so I straight away ruled out the possibility of returning to Ipswich and my job. When I rang Ken to say I was free, he said, 'Come on home!' which is exactly what I did.

Ken lived in a Tudor-style flat in the suburb of New Farm, and worked nights as a drinks waiter. He had some interesting stories to tell, and was also very knowledgeable about wine. I felt quite at home there, and some of the other tenants later became my friends. I went for an interview at one of the many nursing homes in the area and was accepted to start work in two weeks' time.

Notwithstanding, just prior to the start date of my new job, my father and brother arrived one morning at Ken's flat when I was making him breakfast. 'Knock her out!' my father commanded my brother.

Bobby replied, 'She seems all right to me.'

Ken then left saying he was going to ring the police to evict my father and brother. We ended up downstairs, and I was not going to go easily. I very melodramatically jumped in the swimming pool, clothes and all, crying out, 'I'd rather drown than go with you!'

A police lady arrived in response to Ken's call, but in the end, it was I who ended up leaving, and you can guess where I was going—the maximum-security ward.

There I was, at twenty-four years of age, still trapped in a web of parental control and supposed illness!

Chapter 14

It occurs to me that my previous rendition of Osler House may have been too kind, for it did not convey adequately the day-to-day indignities and the frustration I experienced whilst I was there.

Once again, as in Female Eight, in each individual room, there was one large window equipped with a wooden shutter that could be locked over it, blocking out even the moonlight. In some rooms, a metal bed replaced the fixed bed that was bolted to the floor, and there was no other furniture in the room. The same heavy wooden doors closed by the same large key allowed me to continue my contemplations 'from the inside of the keyhole' every night.

The only way a patient could initiate communication with the nursing staff was to call out to them.

There were several garden benches outside in the yard, which was surrounded by a high wire fence that was topped with rolls of razor wire. There were additional rolls of razor wire all along the gutters of the building itself, and there was no other equipment of any kind in the yard.

About twenty feet away from our building and yard was a similar building and yard, which housed the male patients and prisoners transferred from the men's prison. We were not permitted to talk to these patients.

In order to convey some of the atmosphere to you and the daily tension, I am including direct excerpts taken from the Nurses' Daily Report (FOI Notes). Bear in mind that Osler House also housed inmates from the women's prison who had been transferred for psychiatric assessment and treatment. Some of these women had been convicted of very publicized and cruel crimes.

> *27.11.77:* Visited by mother and father 8am—abusive to them. Noisy. Eating and drinking well. Voided in bed. Given Serenace 10mg at 9.10pm
>
> *28.11.77:* Path results noted by Dr Peters. Patient requesting her own clothes etc etc.

30.11.77: IMI [intramuscular injection] Modecate 12.5mg given at 11.15am. Interviewed by Dr Welling. May have yard privileges at staff's discretion. May go to dentist tomorrow with 2 nurse escorts (Dr's instructions) via car, also to have lithium test tomorrow and weekly on Thursdays for next few weeks. Weekly path slip written. Dental app 11.00am tomorrow. Nurses notified re escorts etc.

Treatment—10mgs Mogadon nocte X 1 week, IMI Modecate 12.5 stat of same given. Dr's instructions—patient to remain in ward clothes today and tomorrow, may have own clothes on return from dentist.

1.12.77: To dentist and pathology with 2 nurse escorts via car 10.30am. Returned to ward 11.00am. Phone call from pathology—serum lithium 0.9.

1.12.77: Pinched tomato off patient's (K) plate at evening meal. Then wanted lettuce. Patient(L) asked Margaret, 'Would you like a piece of lettuce?' on which K answered, 'No, let her have it. She might choke on it! On which L threatened K. Then Margaret said: 'Don't take any notice of her, she's a murderess,' on which a fight broke out between the three of them. The alarm bell was rung and each girl was put in her room. Margaret was given IMI Serenace 10mg to settle. Not much effect.

5.12.77: Path slip seen by Dr Peters.

6.12.77: Modecate 2.5mg given this morning. Cogentin given for E.P.S. [extra-pyramidal side effects] Artane 4mg BD [twice per day]. Cogentin 2mls PRN [when needed]. Dr Welling requests Dr Peters to check Serenace dose as he feels it may be too high. Also patient complains of a sore throat.

6.12.77: Seen by Dr Peters re treatment.

8.12.77: No lithium given as test is due. Seen by Dr Welling—transfer to open ward, Noble House B under Category B. Done this morning and Serum Lithium

8.12.77: Recent transfer from Osler House at 1.20pm, Treatment as per transfer notes. NO clothes on and lying in her locker.

8.12.77: Reviewed by Assessment Team this afternoon.

8.12.77: Serum Lithium 0.8 over phone.

9.12.77: Unable to settle, very restless, talking loudly and quite agitated, PRN medication ordered for this patient. Settled late @2am and woke again at 5am.

9.12.77: Seen by Dr Welling. Mogadon 20mg nocte[at night] and Serenace 10mg IMI PRN.

10.12.77: Overactive and talkative. Serenace liquid given at 6am and repeated at 10.30am. This was given orally due to shortage of ampoules.

12.12.77: Pathology for lithium this AM.

12.12.77: Seen by Dr Welling. Treatment change—Lithium Carb 250mg TDS and 500mg Nocte. Melleril Syrup 150mg PRN. Melleril 100mg TDS [three times per day]and Nocte. Artane 2mg BD. Mogadon 20mg Nocte. Cogentin 2mg PRN

Retention of urine—to be catheterized STAT[immediately].

Urine specimen sent to pathology. Path forms completed. Specimen sent to Path. Catheter passed—One litre of urine drained.

I will leave it to my readers to consider the various aspects of this one period out of many under treatment.

PART 2

Accepting the Diagnosis—the Consequences

Chapter 15

The applause seemed deafening as I proudly walked up to the podium to accept the Top of the State Award for Practice and Theory on my graduation night as an enrolled nurse at the Prince Charles Hospital.

My father's face was beaming, and the smile never left my mother's face as the other nurses crowded round to congratulate me. I will always remember my father's words when one friend suggested he must have been surprised when I won the award, and he replied, 'No, I was expecting it!'

As I happily clutched the small pewter jug I'd been given with my certificate, my mind slipped back over the previous year. There wasn't anything sensational or out of the ordinary to recall, and that was a terrific start. The year 1978 had been very good for me, the best so far. I had turned twenty-five in November, was still under the care of a private psychiatrist, and no longer on injections of Modecate (fluphenazine decanoate) or any of the other myriad of drugs I had been on whilst in hospital. My legs were no longer restless and my mind was clear. The only medication I was on was lithium, and I had regular serum lithium tests at a private pathologist.

My parents no longer accompanied me on my appointments, and this alone gave me a lot more confidence. So, by default, I more or less accepted that I could live happily whilst taking lithium. I even began taking driving lessons from a driving school. Previously I'd had only a learner's permit for a motorbike.

I enjoyed being a nurse. I had long since abandoned my plan to become a registered nurse, but what I really liked was being able to make the patients comfortable, and reassuring them by being cheerful and willing to work hard to look after their needs.

Making beds, giving a great back rub, cleaning the pan room—I was happy in all of these roles. This was the real me. I felt a kindness towards my patients, and I applied myself fully to my studies to gain as much knowledge as I could.

I lived in the nurses' quarters, and went to visit Ken twice a week. Yes, he was still in my life, and this was another aspect that kept me feeling happy.

On one occasion, Ken came home to meet my parents. They were polite for once, but didn't give any approval for our relationship. Why didn't that surprise me? I was surprised, though, to come across a letter some time later that my mother had written to 'Jesus' saying how she knew Ken was a bad influence on me, and she was basically praying that we would split up. As usual, I felt overwhelmed by her 'support'.

In spite of this negative input, everything was going fine in my life, and that graduation night marked the high point of all my achievements so far. It was very exciting and rewarding!

I realize that what I have written so far shows a glimpse of the struggles I went through and a little of the triumph, but I have told you very little about myself. Now, I won't go on to relate what I feel are my most endearing qualities, but I do feel that, through my life, I have gained an understanding of people and developed an empathy for those who are suffering or those striving to triumph over injustice or misfortune. I am also very loyal to my friends.

I have been compiling this book over many years, writing about experiences as they happened, or soon after, to capture the important details that would otherwise be lost with the passage of time.

As I am putting together these previous writings and incorporating passages from my Freedom of Information notes, I am basically living in two worlds—the past and the present. I know how my story ends, and how happy I am now, and I am sharing that journey with my readers.

My goal is to give you hope that, no matter how desperate you may feel for yourself or your loved ones, you too may triumph over a diagnosis of manic depression, and your road of discovery may be a lot shorter than mine.

Although I never before shared the contents of this book, the title was well known to my family, as it seemed the most appropriate, and I liked it. My mother once commented that I should be calling the book, *Against All Odds*. This was shortly after I had completed my bachelor of arts with a double major in psychology.

I didn't think too much about her remark at the time, but in 2007, through the Freedom of Information Act, I became aware of information that had previously been hidden from me. This information shocked me, and I realized it had no doubt influenced my parents' perception of my life. Paradoxically, I may have been robbed of some of my greatest achievements, if I had been privy to these facts earlier.

However, that is getting ahead of myself. I will now return to the aftermath of that triumphant night when my family and I felt proud.

Chapter 16

Only Ken did not seem overly impressed with my achievement. In fact, he seemed more interested in the girl from New Zealand who was staying with the tenants next door to him. This, in turn, left me feeling very let down and left out.

I had been looking forward to going on a holiday to Nambour with one of my nursing friends, and Ken had announced quite casually that he would come up about a fortnight after I had arrived there.

As it turned out, this holiday was to raise doubts in my own mind as to whether I did have manic depression. In spite of everything else that had gone before, I always believed I had a reason for my actions, and did not accept the argument to the contrary.

So what was so different about this holiday?

The long-awaited vacation started off happily and very low key, but it was to escalate into a series of strange events.

The night was evil dark, and the wind was wild. Trees overhanging the narrow road were being buffeted into strange shapes, reflected by the occasional headlights of a passing car.

For a short while, a small, mauve-coloured animal like a little elephant seemed to accompany me, and I took this as a good omen or a mysterious sign that I was safe, and that this trip was both logical and acceptable to the hidden world of the night. At the same time, I wondered if this apparition was just my imagination, but I felt reassured and protected.

I was walking quickly with the speed of a power walker. In my memory, it seems as if I was running—'running-walking'—with an inexhaustible energy and determination.

My new blue leather boots—I had just bought them that same day—were tight on my feet, and the three inch heels weren't conducive to my immediate activity. I felt compelled to continue, but apprehensive at the same time.

My destination was a small pub about five miles out of Nambour. This was all I knew—I had never seen this hotel before, but I knew my newly-found friend was the live-in chef at this establishment.

I'd always found it difficult to sleep in a new environment, and the previous ten days had been no exception. I'd been trying to help this process along by not only taking my lithium as prescribed, but adding an extra one here and there, in the hope that this would aid my sleeping and maintain a healthy balance and harmony.

But this was all to no avail, and this night was the culmination of my diminished sleep pattern and my anxiousness to relay a message to Charlie.

When I had first met Charlie, he had told me his friends called him Cookie. This had seemed quite ludicrous to me. I did not associate it with his profession, but with the crunchy biscuits containing peanuts and mixed fruit that my mother used to bake.

That evening, I had decided I wanted to tell him that I could use his nickname—not really a very plausible reason for my night outing.

As Desiderata states, 'Many fears are born of fatigue and loneliness,' and that was never more true than in this case.

I'd been disappointed by Ken's lack of enthusiasm about my nursing award, and lack of sleep had multiplied the importance of pleasing my new friend. I'd told my parents by phone that I was going to break it off with Ken, which was what they had been pressuring me to do all that year.

However, I could hear the anxious tone in their voices when they asked, 'Why are you doing this now? What's wrong? What's happening?' And this made me feel more determined than ever that Charlie would play a big role in my life.

Just that afternoon, I'd been for a walk and picked flowers from people's gardens as I passed by. And not just flowers—I'd picked oranges from trees in the gardens of houses that looked devoid of occupants. I learnt later that someone had spoken to my nursing friend Jenny about this. It had not been dangerous behaviour on my part, but not usual either.

A refreshing night's sleep might have put me back on track, but when daylight faded and I went to bed, the welcome oblivion of slumber refused to join me. After taking two extra lithium tablets and lying still, I only became more restless, and an idea had begun to form in my head that I would go and visit Charlie.

So I carefully dressed, putting on my new boots, and took on the demeanour of a person with a mission—something like a character in a movie where deeper hidden reason is the motivation for adventurous action . . .

Thus, I continued on my way until, eventually, I saw the outline of the pub drawing closer. A new dilemma then confronted me, for the hotel was in darkness—the last drinks had long been served. So there I was, but where would I find Charlie, or 'Cookie'?

All was quiet as I walked to the back of the building. On the second storey, I could see a veranda railing reminiscent of the Old Queenslander style of architecture. I reasoned this would be where he stayed.

The drainpipe coming down from the roof seemed the only way up, and after three or four unsuccessful attempts, I finally managed to gain my footing and climb up to the veranda. This in itself was an incredible physical feat for me, and looking back I wonder how I did it!

An incredible achievement it may have been, but the wisdom behind the whole escapade—very questionable!

Nevertheless, I had come that far, so how could I attract his attention? A couple of small wooden tables were positioned on the veranda; a deck of cards had been carelessly tossed on one of these. There were three doors along the wall of the hotel.

I flicked a few cards around, and being rewarded with no response, moved one of the tables along the floor a little. That certainly got some action—Charlie came out of the middle door. His arm went back into a startled fist on seeing me. He was ready to punch me out! My hasty explanation averted this, but he was not interested in a conversation or anything else with me. He was in major disbelief.

He led me through his room—his washing was hanging on a makeshift line—and then down the darkened staircase. He let me out the front door and pointed me back to the desolate road, to return the way I'd come.

By then I had a different resolve. In some ways I was quite logical: I could understand Charlie being angry and shocked, and I knew I could never explain the reason for my visit. After all, it had been so unnecessary—I would have seen him during the following few days anyway. Now, of course, I would never be able to see him again.

But I still had to get back to our lodgings—a lone figure on a dark, blustery night. This time, I tried to hitch a ride. I stood on the roadway on one occasion in front of the oncoming headlights as a solitary car pulled quickly to a stop—and then sped away. Not until I was nearly halfway back did a couple give me a lift into town. From there, I trudged the rest of the way, by that time cursing my boots and wondering how I was ever going to get them off, for they were feeling extremely tight and uncomfortable!

It was quietly dark when, early in the morning, I returned to my room, still unnoticed. After wrestling my boots off, I followed an unbidden compulsion, took off my clothes, and walked around for about five minutes outside the unit. Even as I was doing this, I knew it was bizarre behaviour, on top of everything else. I then went back to my room and redressed, never mentioning this aspect to anyone.

But I knew something was wrong. Previously, I had embarked upon my adventures as a last resort or the only possible means to an end.

Now I had done something for which there was no good reason or necessity, and behaved strangely as well—not just the 'elephant' and the trip to see Charlie, and walking about without my clothes, but picking flowers and oranges from people's gardens . . . in fact, the whole event!

So, I was quite willing to let Jenny ring my parents. My dad and brother came and picked me up in what my brother described as a very hair-raising trip, with my father very anxious at the wheel. After my recent success, this was unexpected and unwanted!

Although the cry was raised that I wasn't taking my lithium, I knew that wasn't true—far from it. I had been taking extra lithium in the belief that it would grant me the miraculous sleep that I knew I needed.

But had I placed too much faith in lithium—were there hidden dangers lurking there? Accepting the diagnosis had brought with it new difficulties, more of which were to follow.

Miraculously—or ironically—no hospitalization resulted from this experience. I was quietly compliant, made a visit to my private psychiatrist, and I was left to contemplate and regroup. I never saw Cookie or Jenny again.

Chapter 17

As the kaleidoscope of my life continued to turn slowly and the pieces were still scattered, I tried once again to establish order in my life.

Just two months after my holiday to Nambour, I resumed working as an enrolled nurse at a large private hospital, the Wesley, always keeping so much information to myself that I couldn't explain.

It seemed inevitable, then, at the age of twenty-five, nine whole years after my initial diagnosis, that I would have to accept that I had manic depression. There were twists and turns that didn't seem to make any sense, and I was acutely aware of this.

Even though I was living onsite in nurses' quarters, my parents were very intent on 'keeping an eye' on my every action. Once again, I was under very close scrutiny from afar. Six months passed, and my parents claimed they could see 'signs' that my health was deteriorating—and then the pressure was on!

Do you know how hard it is to stay logical and focused when other people are making conclusions and assumptions about everything and anything you do—even actions they are in agreement with, such as my eventual parting from Ken?

In the previous nine years, I had made several attempts, one with a doctor's supervision, to cease medication, in particular lithium, which had been my permanent long-term medication. However, this had never been done over a long period of time in peaceful surroundings, which was what I had concluded was necessary when coming off medication.

At all other times, I was compliant, and after my success at the Prince Charles, I felt I could still achieve in spite of taking the medication. In fact, I then began to place too much reliance on lithium.

This was what happened when I was working at the Wesley. My parents' constant criticism of my lifestyle totally disturbed my sleep pattern, and I tried to counteract this by taking more lithium. After all, wasn't this the method the doctors themselves prescribed? But once again, this combination resulted in my admission to Lowson House.

If my reliance on lithium wasn't becoming problematic, any stay in hospital constantly reinforced the doctors' perception that more and more medication was necessary for any desired result. Just how much medication can a person absorb and still be monitored according to a scale of normal responses?

During my eight-week stay in Lowson House, the senior psychiatrist, Dr Musgrave, had allowed my lithium to rise to an unprecedented level of 1.7, and I was, not surprisingly, displaying toxic symptoms. In conjunction with this, I was on a massive amount of Serenace (haloperidol), so much so that I was completely disorientated all of the time and could not even find my own bed or attend to my own personal hygiene. At this stage, my parents became alarmed by the severity of this treatment regime. As well, shock treatment (electroconvulsive therapy, or ECT) had been suggested, but my father had continued to steadfastly and adamantly refuse his permission.

My parents wanted me to transfer to Barrett Centre, which was the more modern hospital that had replaced some of the wards of the antiquated Wolston Park, located in its adjoining grounds. For once, we were in complete agreement.

So, against the advice of my psychiatrist at Lowson House, and with my parents' approval, I signed myself out.

In Dr Musgrave's transfer letter to the doctor in charge at Barrett Centre, he concluded that, on leaving, I had no signs of psychosis, and if anything, my affect was a bit 'flat'. (FOI Notes)

When I arrived at Barrett Centre on 13 June 1980, I was described as pleasant, cooperative, and of quiet demeanour. My answers to the usual stock questions were recorded as above average, although I had some difficulty in producing words. I was also very drowsy, and my lithium level was still elevated at 1.2. (FOI Notes)

My intake of lithium was then reduced to four tablets a day. As I had had so much Serenace with devastating effect at Lowson House, I requested Melleril as an alternative when I was at Barrett Centre, but as the daily transcript reveals, a treatment plan based on 'more and more' medication resulted in even further distress.

After two weeks at Barrett Centre:

> *27/06/80:* Given IMI Serenace at 2.05pm. Treatment changes as per tracydex. Given Melleril syrup 100mg 3/24 at 3.05pm, 6.05pm and 9.05pm.

28/06/80: Very disturbed and overtalkative, asking for Melleril—given Melleril syrup at 7.45am.

Still extremely agitated and disturbing the whole ward. Melleril syrup given at 10.45pm with effect.

Patient very elated and active. During dinner, her activity and short temper caused concern. PRN Melleril syrup 100mg given at 5pm and patient placed in seclusion. Patient took a good deal of time to settle during which she urinated in wardrobe.

Returned to day area at 7pm, patient condition deteriorated and a separate dose of Melleril syrup 100mg was given.

11pm—patient aggressive and demanding from 10pm. Restless, continually moving about, demanding writing material, medication and asking questions, refused to put out light. Given Melleril syrup 100mg at 11pm., continuing to generally make a nuisance of herself, wandering into office and male dormitory. Locked in her Room at 12.45am. Given Melleril syrup at 2am with no effect, knocking on door, calling out, demanding instant attention.

Melleril syrup repeated at 5am.

29/06/80: Sleeping on floor until 9am. Then awake and was as disturbed as previously. Urinated in locker drawer. After PRN medication, at 9.15am, mood was still labile but settled after a few minutes of swearing and screaming.

Still agitated at 12 midday. Given 100mg Melleril syrup PRN at 12.00md.

Agitated still at 1.30pm. Slamming staff recess door, abusive towards staff. Given 100mg PRN Melleril at 1.30pm.

Disturbed behaviour of patient, excitement, temper. Required PRN medication given at 4.30pm.

> Not as disturbed this PM. Mood swings at times, mildly aggressive. Visited by mother and father, who had to leave when patient became tearful.
>
> *30/06/80:* Mood swings, pressure of speech, negative at times.
>
> Awake all night. Talking incessantly, angry at times, room in utter chaos, dress inappropriate. Melleril syrup given 1.00am with no effect. Given pan when room locked—used same.

A few days later:

> *03/07/80:* Parents interviewed by Dr Roberts. They feel they know when Margaret is getting 'high' and doctor agrees that this is probably true, although he did caution against their request for an increased dosage of lithium re the possible damage to Margaret's kidneys. S/lithium 1.00. Dr would like to repeat S/lithium tomorrow. Melleril syrup given at 5pm—next due at 11pm please. Voided in bed at 6pm—all bed linen and blanket changed.

Six days later:

> *09/07/80:* Condition remains same. Verbally aggressive. Complaining that she is being given the wrong dose of medication. Irritable and easily distracted. Settled to bed early
>
> *10/07/80*: To dentist at 1pm, irritable and unwilling to co-operate, states dentist ruined her teeth before and is scared to go. Speech very slurred.
>
> Filling attended to by dentist.
>
> Serun Lithium level 1.35. Dr Robert's instruction to withhold lithium for 24 hours. Then take each day except Sunday.

Visited by parents this evening; walked away from parents and went to watch TV. Later rejoined parents and spoke with them before they left.

11/07/80: Sitting in chair most of morning, some interaction with other patients—conversation sometimes inappropriate. Appears happy.

These entries over a two-week period serve to illustrate the whole general trend of high doses, including, once again, a very toxic level of lithium.

25/07/80: Very noisy and disruptive this am. Upsetting others. Patient given Largactil (chlorpromazine hydrochloride) 75mg this afternoon.

Missing from ward at noon. Barrett Centre and Wolston Park grounds searched by ward staff. Dr Stafford notified, will consult with Dr Roberts.

1.40pm mother phoned—not at home—feels that Margaret had gone to Brisbane on business or to Wolston Park to visit a friend.

I returned of my own volition to the ward at 3.30pm and was transferred to a more secure ward in Barrett Centre.
One week later:

01/08/80: Lithium 0.9

Mr Oliver wants transfer to different psychiatrist. Refuses to let Margaret have ECT. Margaret seems much better this morning. Patient tried to chuck tablets at nurse—says she doesn't think the tablets are good for her.'

What do you think?

Chapter 18

The Moving finger writes; and, having writ,
Moves on: nor all your Piety nor Wit
Shall lure it back to cancel half a Line,
Nor all your Tears wash out a Word of it.[2]*

As many people do, I tried to justify to myself everything I did by constructive argument to and fro. Most of the time this sufficed to convince me that I always strove to behave in a rational and realistic manner, but the disturbing factor, which I very rarely dwelt on or even admitted to myself, was what I shall refer to collectively as 'bizarre events'. This was behaviour of my own, which I kept almost exclusively to myself and for my reflection alone. I couldn't explain this behaviour; indeed, I would never have believed it possible. It had nonetheless taken place—and I was the primary witness.

As I put pen to paper, I am even now reluctant to mention some of these incidents. However, it was these very events that led me to persist in my quest to discover whether or not I really did have manic depression. Without these incidents, I could believe that cause and effect explained the kaleidoscope of my life.

Looking back over the whole period on later reflection, I was able to recognize a pattern that preceded these events, but for now, I will relate the incidents as they occurred.

The night escapade in Nambour was the first of these four incidents. The next episode, which occurred four years later, certainly caused a lot of concern, but once again, no one knows the whole story but me—and now, you.

My friend, Belle, and I had not seen each other for fourteen years, since we had been cadet nurses together. Belle had already done some travelling overseas, and one day, out of the blue, she rang and asked me if I would like to go on a holiday to Singapore and Hong Kong with her.

At first, I thought that would be the last place I'd like to go, but the idea grew on me, and my parents were in agreement as everything had

---

[2] * *The Rubaiyat of Omar Khayam* translation by Edward J. Fitzgerald 1859

been going smoothly for over three years, and I had just successfully completed a child health assistant course at the local Maternal and Child Health Home in Ipswich.

So Belle and I received a happy farewell from Brisbane International Airport and arrived in Singapore after a ten-hour flight. Despite the fact that I had difficulty sleeping in a new environment, Belle and I spent four terrific days in Singapore. We had fun and enjoyed ourselves touring, haggling with shop owners, buying gifts, trying the authentic local cuisine, and taking photos. We tasted a little of the culture of Singapore and observed the very vigilant officers of the law who, by their presence ensured Singapore's spotless environment. There were very forbidding fines if you so much as dropped a cigarette butt on the ground.

A man named Chicolota pedalled Belle and I on a tour of some of the best sights in Singapore. This was no mean effort, for neither of us was a lightweight. We travelled in fine style down the famed Boogie Street where we were offered some interesting photos for purchase. In another spot in Boogie Street, we heard a sad wailing—mourning for a loved one who had passed away.

We made friends with the resident band in our hotel—the Nu Faces—and they later sent us over a copy of their record, hoping we might be able to promote it in Australia.

After our brief but happy stay in Singapore, we boarded China Airlines and arrived at our final destination, Hong Kong.

As soon as Belle and I hit Hong Kong, I knew I was going to love it: the chaotic traffic situation, the shopping, the nightclub dancing . . . but most of all, the people from all walks of life and all countries—a veritable crossroad of culture. But it was also to be my downfall, as I ended up in a strange hospital surrounded by people speaking in an alien tongue.

I know that to this day, Belle has no idea what triggered off the chain of events that were to follow. Only many years later could I look back and put any real reason to my actions.

We had both made friends, and I was pleased to have some positive attention, as I'd had a very hurtful breakup with someone not very long before we'd left Australia.

Belle and I had different likes and dislikes on a holiday. Belle liked shopping bus trips, and was really keen to go to China, which I wasn't. I was happy if I could venture out into the city of Hong Kong on foot and find my way back to the hotel again—I was more interested in the people.

I had been on several of these walking outings, sightseeing in the city. At first, I really enjoyed it, but then I began to notice certain people in the street and in our hotel who seemed to me to have crazed 'demon' eyes, as though possessed, and I felt scared by these people.

On the night in question, Belle had gone out dancing, and I was filling the bath when there was a knock on the door.

I opened the door.

It was one of those people with the devil's eyes, which seemed to look right into me, and I got the fright of my life at seeing him standing there. He was one of the porters of the hotel. I had seen him before and I did not like him at all. I drew in my breath, and said quickly in a low, terrified voice, 'What are you doing here?' And then I screamed at him, 'Go away!'

He went—but I was completely unnerved, and I double-locked the door so nobody could get in. I didn't know what was going on with these people or what was wrong with them, but I felt very frightened. When I went into the bedroom, I saw all the souvenir dragons and dolls Belle had bought. I half remembered hearing, on one of those early-morning evangelist shows on television that these dolls were really idols. I thought that they might be the reason for these people I was seeing, and why I was feeling so afraid. So I broke them all into little pieces . . . snapped off their arms and legs and heads. They were full of spikes and sharp points and awful things. I felt I was right in destroying these idols.

Because I was angry that my girlfriend had bought these disturbing gifts, which were so colourful on the outside but so dangerous in every other way, I broke her camera and destroyed some of her prize film. After that, I just sat on the floor surrounded by the broken pieces.

When Belle returned, she could not get in because I had double-locked the door. But what was I to do? How could I explain to her why I had destroyed her presents? How could I explain to her what I had been experiencing when I couldn't understand any of it myself?

The phone was ringing, but I would not answer it.

The events that followed were traumatic—the hotel's security guards were knocking on my door. Finally, I unlocked the door and let them in. They were armed, weapons drawn, and very unsympathetic when they saw the state of the room. They transported me, handcuffed, to a police station, where a lady police officer interviewed me. Because she couldn't understand me and I couldn't understand her, there wasn't much communication between us, and I became quite abusive.

I was placed in a holding cell that contained only a narrow bench. There were two observation levels high above this cell from which I could be observed.

Since I had not been in contact with Belle since we nursed together, she was not aware that I had a psychiatric history. This may not have been fair on my part, but it was not something I advertised, and I had not foreseen this situation. Besides which, I had been taking my medication faithfully.

Even when I was in the holding cell, I still had my handbag, which contained my lithium. I swallowed two tablets without water to make sure I didn't miss taking them when they were due. If any of you have ever tasted lithium, you will appreciate how determined I was, for it tastes vile. In retrospect, I often wondered why they had actually let me keep my handbag with me. If they had looked inside, they would have found the letter from my doctor outlining my condition and explaining the medication I was carrying—but they did not seem interested in the contents of my bag.

After telephoning my parents to tell them what had happened, Belle found out about my history, and in view of the whole situation, as I found out later, felt very betrayed.

Meanwhile, I was transported to a large metropolitan hospital where they removed the handcuffs.

Up until then, I had remained relatively calm and passive, all the while keeping a tight grip on my handbag containing my passport, my airline ticket home, my lithium, and my money.

One certain nurse was particularly aggravating and unkind to me. I couldn't understand her language or that of anyone else around me, but she was taunting me. What she was really saying I don't know, but it sounded to me in English, like, 'We are going to strip the flesh off your arms and make you eat it!'

It was at this point that I decided to put up some resistance.

I was being carried on a stretcher through what looked like a laboratory. I suddenly reached out and swept the glass apparatus onto the floor, where it shattered into hundreds of pieces.

I then received a 'gentle' injection from my 'favourite' nurse as I was held forcibly down. The rings I was wearing were then ripped from my fingers, the handcuffs were put on again, and chains were applied that pinned me to the stretcher. As a final statement, when they secured the chains, they twisted my left arm in a very painful position—they then left me alone for what seemed like a very long time.

I kept trying to untwist my arm and was just agonized with the pain when the nurses finally returned. And then—relief—they removed the handcuffs and the chains.

'Well, that's an improvement,' I thought out loud. But to myself, I was wondering, *What happens next?*

Chapter 19

Almost immediately, I found myself escorted to an ambulance van. There were already five other patients in the van along with two male nurses as supervisors.

I wasn't sure where we were going, because I hadn't heard a word of English since I left the hotel. It turned out we were en route to Castle Peak Hospital in the New Territories of Hong Kong. This was a psychiatric hospital.

It was night-time when we arrived, and I hadn't eaten all day. The first thing I discovered at this fine establishment was the shortage of food and drink. I couldn't believe it. I arrived at suppertime and was given a plastic mug filled only a third of the way with skim milk, and a piece of unbuttered, sliced bread, which did little to assuage my hunger. However, the girls in my ward were very friendly and generous and gave me some of theirs, not that they had any more than I.

Some of the patients could speak a little English, and I asked them the name of this place. They told me everyone called it the 'snakepit'.

There were only female nurses in the ward, and not long after my arrival, I was offered a large tablet of Largactil (chlorpromazine hydrochloride) which had always seriously affected my ability to think. So I refused it, and they decided to give me an injection instead. It took several of these small nurses to hold me down. I had no objection to taking my customary dose of lithium.

My only other memory of my first night, which I shall never forget, concerned the beds. The bed frames were made of metal, and had been subjected so much use, there was a permanent, large dip in the centre of every one. The meagre mattresses conformed to this same shape. One well-worn blanket provided little warmth, and another sleepless night followed.

However, the snakepit was to become, in a way, my haven.

We wore uniforms that were like pyjama pants and top. They were secured by a continuous cord, and I had some 'accidents' before I learnt the trick of doing them up and undoing them

Everyone walked around with a plastic mug that contained a face washer, toothbrush, toothpaste and soap, as well as toilet paper. This became my custom also.

It was only once every three days that we could have a bath, and even then, it was not in the usual manner. By this, I mean that the bath was filled with about six inches of lukewarm water. We did not sit in the bath, but stood alongside, about four of us at a time. We took a dipper of water and poured it over ourselves. Then we washed using a small piece of soap. We then took another dipper of water to rinse. Finally, we dried ourselves with well-worn towels, which we shared. Even though it was somewhat skimpy, I did look forward to bath day!

I also made attempts at their spoken language and picture script, learned to count to ten, and became a little adept at copying their language symbols.

'What was that?' I thought aloud on my first visit to the loo. The snakepit did not seem to live up to its name as far as snakes were concerned, but I soon became very familiar with the many big, fat rats running around on long furry legs. They resided mainly in the toilet section, which was the only place we could smoke—if we had any cigarettes—which I didn't . . . only the butts of the other inmates. I remember being so much in need of a full cigarette that I grabbed one of the girls by the throat and ordered her to give me one—which she wouldn't. I was rather ashamed of that act of mine, but she forgave me, and after that we became friends.

The other inmates thought I was a novelty, and were forever touching my 'little' nose and stroking my long hair—they were fascinated by me.

During the day when we were inside, we were all in the one room. The constant talking created quite a noise, because conversation had to be loud enough to be heard above the television, which was always on.

The girls were always friendly and kind, and helped me learn the daily routine. However, it was the nights that I found the most difficult. There were not enough beds for everyone, and this discrepancy was 'remedied' by the use of stretchers. I found the beds so warped that I couldn't sleep on them, and one night I begged a particularly nice sister for the use of a stretcher. The first stretcher I set up and lay on collapsed under my not-inconsiderable weight, causing much laughter from everyone else! They then brought me a sturdier one, which took the strain as long as my head hung over one end and my freezing feet hung over the other end. How I wished I was back in my uncomfortable bed! Everyone else thought the whole situation was hilarious, and to add insult to injury, they nicknamed me 'Stinky Feet'.

The meals were pathetic, and invariably consisted of over-cooked cabbage and rice. I soon learnt how to use chopsticks to eat anything I was given. I can remember one really nice meal, though, and that was spareribs, and I was even allowed a second helping—a very unusual practice.

We used to go out into the garden yard during the day. A few of the girls spoke to me in English. I found out that some people lived in the hospital because they couldn't afford to live on the outside. There were three levels for living and three corresponding rates of payment. I was on the lowest level at the cheapest rate.

When we were not in the yard, we were engaged in making Christmas decorations. This was a very fiddly occupation that included tying a knot at the end of some fine, tinselly, gold thread. We also put together plastic flower patterns.

I must also mention the Adairs. They were the assistant nurses, who did all the basic nursing duties, mainly making beds and supervising the making of the decorations. However, if you helped the Adairs make the beds, you would be given two or three cigarettes. I liked that.

One night, I had a surprise. As I waited up for my night-time medication to help me sleep, I saw a very unusual sight outside. It was a religious ceremony. A pig was being roasted on a spit, and money was being burnt as an offering to the participants' God.

A smiling Adair brought me some of the hot, sizzling pork. It was very welcome as I was always hungry, and it was very tasty also.

After I had been there for almost a week, the superintendent of the hospital visited me to see how I was settling in. He was a very courteous man.

My doctor, Dr Lee, was a gentle and very dedicated man, who treated me like a person, and even told me he had become a doctor after he had seen a man who was mentally ill being badly treated and abused at a railway station

The Australian ambassador was also very helpful and kind and visited me twice a week. It seemed to me that I was in a safe place surrounded by friendly people. I was treated very well, and kept up correspondence with my favourite nurse in my ward for four years after my return to Australia.

After two and a half weeks, I was given permission to leave. The ambassador had my luggage delivered to the hospital. My leather handbag that I had held close to me through all the traumatic events before my admission was also given back to me. I felt inside the base of the bag, and there, neatly camouflaged, was my wallet. With some of the money, I was able to pay for my stay in hospital.

The ambassador had arranged my flight home, and he and his young daughter came to the hospital early in the evening to drive me to the airport. I remember my mixed emotions as we took the long drive and I noticed the reflections of the myriad of lights as we approached the airport.

We then sat in the private departure lounge talking. Lost in conversation, we realized with shock that we had missed the announcement that my plane was boarding. Thus, my final memory of Hong Kong is running to board my plane. I made it just in time and was the last passenger to be shown to my seat. The lights flashed, 'Fasten Your Seatbelt', and my holiday was over.

Chapter 20

The plane trip home from Hong Kong was uneventful, with plenty of time for contemplation. When it came right down to it, I didn't really want to go back—the questions would start immediately and go on and on. This return, more or less in disgrace, had not been part of my original plan at all, as you may imagine. I was not ashamed, but more than a little apprehensive.

I was thoroughly exhausted on touch down at Brisbane International Airport, and the world seemed to be spinning slowly around me as the effects of jet lag weighed upon me.

My family may have been more understanding than I had anticipated, but I had just about convinced myself that this was going to be an ordeal. I can only imagine how difficult and agonizing the whole situation must have been for them from thousands of miles away via a few international phone calls.

It was beyond their comprehension why I would destroy Belle's camera and souvenirs, and I could not even try to explain. All such attempts, including one to my mother's minister, were futile. I was very grateful to my parents, though, because they had paid Belle for the damage I had caused, for I knew how disappointed she would have been, and this caused me much regret.

On the other hand, everyone was amazed to find that, before all this happened, I had bought some lovely gifts for my family and friends including an exquisite Rado watch for my father with twelve small, sparkling diamonds marking the hour.

The following day, my father and I, medical certificate in hand, visited our local general practitioner, Dr Burnett. He summarized my condition in a referral to a specialist, noting that I was stabilized on six tablets of 250 mg lithium per day and that a serum lithium level of '1' was considered my optimal level. Dr Burnett noted in his letter that, 'her father is a little difficult in this direction as he does not like these high doses.'

When I read this in my FOI notes, I began to see the pattern whereby, in spite of everything, my father was the one who always seemed to be safeguarding my health, if I could put it that way. In addition, he had never given permission for me to have shock treatment, although it had been suggested on more than one occasion.

Dr Burnett described me as 'a little high' and put me on an additional medication, the same one I had refused in Castle Peak Hospital—Largactil (chlorpromazine hydrochloride). As such, this was very likely a contributing factor to my feeling in a daze and unable to settle down or find any peace.

So the relatively cheerful person who left Hong Kong became more and more depressed. Although when I first arrived back, I tried to remain upbeat and visit several of my friends from work, the real problem was that I could not reconcile this bizarre series of events even to myself.

Although I had no faith in the hospital treatment in Australia, after talking to my aunty and uncle about how I felt, I admitted myself as a voluntary patient to the more modern Barrett Centre I had last been in. I gained some small measure of comfort talking to a reassuring male nurse, but I was on a downward spiral. Whingey, depressed, but compliant, I was much easier to relate to, with none of my usual fire and rebellion.

'Come forward if you need to receive healing, not through my power, but through the power of God!' My very depressed state had led me to turn to other avenues, and my mother and I were attending a healing service led by a man who had developed his faith and healing ability whilst serving a prison sentence for armed hold up, Dr Steve Ryder. He spoke with an understanding of people and life, and there was an optimism at his services that I liked.

I did go out for healing and 'fell down' when he touched me and prayed over me. I came away with a feeling of acceptance of myself, and a refreshed belief that I could once again move forwards. Maybe achievement and happiness were still a possible part of my destiny.

My discharge came soon after, and the clock of time kept ticking. With dull monotony, I attended outpatients, firstly on a fortnightly basis, and then monthly. My medication was evaluated, and serum lithium tests also became a monthly routine. Regularly my mood elevation was recorded, alongside my sleep patterns, my relationship with my parents and friends, and my study progress.

I had abandoned my work goals, and, at my father's suggestion, was studying my senior certificate by correspondence. At first it was very difficult to get used to preparing assignments again, having left school fourteen years previously. However, I persevered, and the following year, I sat the examination in the local TAFE (Technical and Further Education), and was delighted to receive a tertiary entrance score of 975.

The most incapacitating feature of this period was the blurred vision caused by my medication. I often felt that I was about to fall down the stairs I was descending, and only mind over matter prevented this. When I was studying, I wore an old pair of my father's glasses, which just suited my 'temporarily altered' vision.

As I began to achieve in my studies, my battered self-esteem received a boost. My parents allowed me to take lessons for my license using their car, and eventually, at age thirty-two, I obtained my driving license. The eye test for my license was problematic, because as I stood before the chart, I realized that I could not see the letters at all clearly. With uncustomary good fortune, I noticed that the supervising attendant was very involved with another matter at the same time, and paying my efforts very little attention. With a bravado I did not feel, I simply called out the letters I could not see in a confident way, and miraculously received a positive nod. My father, who had accompanied me, looked at me in a quizzical way asking, 'Which line were you reading?' I just smiled, and on unknowing trust, he was silent, leaving it to me to explain later.

Now, I was able to drive myself to and from appointments, and that was a very good feeling in itself. Eventually, I was taken off all other drugs, but the amount of lithium I was taking remained high. This was to become a critical factor.

Meanwhile, the winds of good fortune were buffeting me from other directions.

A short time prior to my trip to Hong Kong, my father and I had approached an elderly lady who was sitting on a bench at an interstate bus depot in my hometown of Ipswich. A large white suitcase sat beside her. 'You must be Aunty Annie,' I observed with a smile.

She replied in the warm, characteristic voice I remembered from my childhood, 'And you must be Margaret.'

Those few simple words were the prelude to a friendship that was to endure over many years and in many different situations. Aunty Annie was really my mother's aunty—my great-aunty. She had known my mother and her siblings and been part of their lives as they grew up. At seventy years of age, she was starting a new adventure by moving to Queensland, having sold her plant nursery at the foot of Mt Macedon in Victoria. This was a very fortuitous time for the sale, as the whole street in which her nursery had been located was destroyed in the Ash Wednesday fires just a year later.

It was also very beneficial for me, in that Aunty Annie built a lovely little house just a five-minute walk from where our family lived.

By a strange twist of fate, it turned out that both of us had very similar interests. Aunty Annie liked trinkets and jewellery as did I. We could go shopping, trying on pretty dresses for hours, and over the years we used to travel to Brisbane to do our Christmas shopping together.

Playing duets on the piano gave us a lot of pleasure. When I was at home studying, I would go down to her place most days and watch the 'soapies'.

Smoking was permitted in her lounge room, which wasn't the case at home, and I could talk to her. But most importantly, she believed in me—she didn't have to put it into words. I knew.

My aunty attended church regularly. However, unlike many people who did the same, she was what I liked to term a 'practical Christian'. She was prepared to be there for people who needed help or support, and over the years became an aunt to many unrelated friends. She practiced a gentle wisdom without judgement.

Chapter 21

Four years had elapsed since my unceremonious return from Hong Kong. I had kept up correspondence with my favourite nurse from the Castle Peak Hospital and looked forward to her letters. During this time I was clinically well, and relationships were good at home.

There was a very happy period when I stayed with a friend of mine who was about to have twins. I was, for her, a kind of live-in help during the weeks preceding the birth. We had worked together at the Maternal and Child Health Home and had maintained our friendship over the ensuing years. I valued her trust and felt that my life was coming together again. But there was an underlying tension that was about to come to a head.

By this time, my friends were mainly those I had met in hospital. I understood and related to them, and they accepted me as well. We also had shared experiences in hospital.

My parents had an uneasy acceptance of Daniel, who used to visit occasionally whilst I was studying, and we would go swimming and have a picnic lunch every Saturday. He gave me a simple pearl ring for my birthday, but when the pearl became loose, I put the ring away for safekeeping.

As a replacement, Daniel gave me a beautiful, three-piece, flower-shaped sapphire ring that I wore with pride, but my parents felt I could do better in my choice of a man.

Another friend whom I had met in hospital was Jo who lived with her friend, Tania in Blackstone, about four miles from my home. I liked to visit when I could and we often reminisced—over a cup of coffee—about the times we had shared in hospital.

During this time, I also began attending the little Welsh church near Jo's place. I found the people to be so genuine, warm, and friendly, and they made Jo and me very welcome. Twenty years later, I was to return to this very church to be married.

My parents could never understand why I liked the company of my friends from the hospital so much, and increasingly they tried to restrict my seeing them, claiming they had a bad influence on me.

Although Aunty Annie had no problem meeting my friends and welcoming them into her home, they were certainly not tolerated under any circumstance at my family home. As more and more pressure was put on me to stay away from my friends, I saw my small window of hope being closed.

My FOI notes confirm how all of this was beginning to take its toll on me:

> Presents as agitated ++ ; teary at times; some pressure of speech; settled during interview.
>
> Otherwise: coping very well; helping recuperating friend of her mother's with housework; has had some recent difficulties—boyfriend is an in-patient now, recent flare up of his medical condition, and not accepted by her parents.
>
> After discussion, patient did not want admission, nor do I think it is warranted.

My readers may also appreciate that this whole situation was one I recognized as very dangerous—notes like 'easy to tears' placed me in a very vulnerable position. So, it was agreed that my lithium dosage would be increased by one 250mg tablet (500mg twice a day and 750mg at night) and I would return for my next visit in two months.

An uneasy period followed.

From my point of view, I was just trying to live my life, but always there was a negative acceptance of this. As usual I felt I was trying to be squeezed into a mould that was not fitted for me.

With Daniel in hospital, I wanted to be supportive, but could not even visit. If I wished to see Jo and Tania, it was a battle: 'You can see your friends too often,' was the way my mother saw it. It was at this point that desperation became my greatest hurdle.

I was so angry that I made a vow to myself: I would write down all the events from the beginning in an effort to sort out the facts from the fiction, to try and make sense of it—analyse it more closely and honestly—to determine the cause and effect and look at the snowballing action, my continued resentment, and whether or not I could ever envisage a smooth future.

Over the next week, I wrote a twenty-page history on foolscap. Just reliving and thinking about everything that had happened seriously upset my sleep patterns. I have already voiced many of my conclusions in this book, but perhaps the most telling conclusion concerned my feelings about lithium: 'It has never been proven to me that lithium helps,' I wrote, 'but I know that just going straight off it is no good, and no test.' By contrast, I also clung to the hope that, if I was taking my lithium as prescribed, everything should be all right.

As such, it was an emotionally charged, but lithium compliant, woman who defiantly walked the few miles to Jo and Tania's house. They were sympathetic to my feelings and offered to let me stay there.

I was unnerved by my brother's 'expected visit' that evening, and his stand that I should come back home. This just made me feel more under pressure and threat. Would I never be the owner of my life? *More importantly*, I thought, *I will be having my bi-monthly serum lithium tomorrow, which should prove to everyone that I am taking my recently increased dosage of lithium—so shouldn't everything be fine if my level is right?*

The following morning, I smoothed my hands over the lovely silk skirt and fresh blouse Jo had lent me for the day. I was catching a taxi and train to the hospital. Of course, I'd had another almost-sleepless night in the face of all these events.

Nevertheless, I had a sample of my blood taken for analysis, and went to the local shopping centre to fill in time till I saw the doctor for my results. Although I was feeling tired as I sat at the coffee shop, I had no premonition or any idea at all of my next actions. I was sitting alone and had ordered toasted sandwiches and an iced coffee. After I finished my meal, I sat observing the people at the other tables, and those walking past, as I often did. For some reason, which I couldn't understand or explain, I began undoing my blouse, which I then removed. I then took off my bra and tossed it over the railing near where I was sitting on the first floor. I was aware of *what* I was doing, but not *why*.

When a security guard came up to me with my discarded clothing, I somehow regained my composure and told him I was on my way to see a doctor at the nearby psyche hospital. I was allowed to leave. I then took myself back to the hospital for the results of my test. Although the result was 'good' (8.5), and I seemed perfectly 'recovered', I instigated my own admission—for these were events I could not explain to myself (or mention to anyone else!)

But I was left wondering and in complete bewilderment of my own actions. I felt more uneasy about this than I had about any previous event.

In some ways, hospitalization in an open ward provided opportunities that life on the outside did not. For instance, I could spend the whole day with fellow patients and friends, I could visit the canteen, I could smoke, and I could walk around the grounds.

It was during this period that I became friends with the chaplain of the hospital who lived in the hospital grounds. He gave a service each Sunday, and I became his organist. I renewed this interesting connection many years later in a much happier situation.

I always liked to believe that, amongst my hospital friends, I could maintain a sense of humour when presenting my life situation. I have found that no matter how many times I have been able to contemplate 'from the inside of the keyhole', I have never been able to get used to it, and if I couldn't sleep in a locked room despite medication, I endured a long and tortured night. Although in the more modern Barrett Centre where I was then, there were no wooden shutters on the windows, and everything was quite pleasant, there was still that lock on the door.

The following incident really appealed to my sense of humour. I had worked out a theory, and this night I had the opportunity to put it into action. Sometimes, the staff would lock the door as soon as they let me in, and other times they would let me go to the bathroom first. They would then come back and check the door before locking it.

On this occasion, I went to the bathroom, and on my return, I broke a small part off a wooden ornament I had in my room. I wedged this small piece of wood securely under the door.

As I expected, when they checked the door, they thought it was already locked. So after a little while, when the activity in the outside ward lessened, I bunched up my bedclothes to look like my own form sleeping.

Next, I crept out of my room and went to visit a friend of mine, and sat on the floor next to her bed. She went to the bathroom, and I climbed into the wardrobe to avoid being seen.

I was going to give myself up, but then I had a better idea. When my friend returned, she went straight to bed, and after I had hastily discussed my plan with her, I went back into the wardrobe.

It was about three in the morning, and I was getting a little cramped, but I was determined to see this through. There was a great flurry of activity when the alert staff discovered I wasn't in my 'locked room'.

They were switching on lights and calling my name. I, of course, was feeling quite smug! When they came to the room where I was secreted, I forcefully pushed open the door of the wardrobe and bounded out!

They were dumbfounded, and their consternation and disbelief contrasted with my laughter!

They went away to prepare their answer to everything, but the look on their faces was reward enough. I hardly felt the injection, and then I was 'more securely' locked up.

Chapter 22

On a more serious note, one of the main problems I had with being in hospital was that they plied me with a lot more drugs, once I was there, than I would have when I was not in hospital. Also present were the undesirable side effects, which I have described before, and always there was some new drug they wanted to introduce into my regimen.

During my previous stay in hospital, I had been encouraged to take an anti-epileptic drug, carbamazepine, as part of my treatment. After my release, my father accompanied me on an outpatient appointment to discuss this. The doctor was stressing there were only minimal, if any, side effects; indeed, the drug was considered quite safe. At this point, my father opened the medical journal he had brought with him and slammed it down on the desk in front of the alarmed doctor, asking in a demanding voice, 'So what do you have to say about this?' There, in graphic detail, was an exposition of this very drug, with shocking illustrations of severely damaged and bleeding gums caused by this treatment.

I was never troubled with any further suggestions regarding this drug, and I was reassured that the bond between my father and me was still there in spite of all we'd been through. I was very impressed that he would stand up for me like that, and in such a radical way. My father was very knowledgeable about matters that interested him, and over the years he had read a great deal on the treatment of manic depression. Since my hospitalization in 1980, with two incidents of serious toxicity at both Lowson House and Barrett Centre, he had been opposed to high levels of lithium, even though the doctors thought this was the only way of controlling my condition.

As I put together the pages of this book, I often wonder how any life continued for the rest of my family with all the turmoil and confrontation surrounding my own life. But one large contributing factor to this turmoil was the conflict of personalities in our home. My father had spent twenty years in the Royal Australian Air Force (RAAF) and had served in 'signals' during World War II and the Korean War. He left the service with a rank of warrant officer, and was thus accustomed to giving instructions and having them followed.

On leaving the air force, he had worked as a chemist at Tennyson Power Station, and finally as timekeeper at Swanbank Power Station. I had always been very proud of my father, and this had also been a factor when he had started questioning my behaviour in my teens. However, my father kept his own counsel and did not sway with the breeze. I had always liked his saying: 'I'm not always right, but I'm never wrong.'

My mother was also a very hard worker, and worked alongside my father painting, gardening, cooking, and cleaning. Her hands were rough and worn, attesting to this. She was highly regarded by her friends, and with them she seemed to have a generosity and understanding of their life situations that she was never able to share with me. She regularly donated money to charities such as the Bible Society and overseas missions.

Up until my mother first went to hospital, we had shared a good relationship.

After her hospitalization, my mother became more deeply entrenched in religion, but it seemed to be based on fear and unresolved guilt. However, she was very genuine in her faith, and attended study classes and prayer meetings, and also underwent adult baptism to pledge her conviction.

With me she was always anxious, worried, and expecting the worst. My mother had her way of looking at things and tried to extend this to my way of thinking. 'Whatever happened to my lovely little girl?' she wondered aloud one day.

I retorted, 'You did!' but she never understood why I showed resentment and anger.

Personally, I felt very closely aligned to the words of one of Slim Dusty's most well-renowned songs:

> And the biggest disappointment in the family was me,
> The only twisted branch upon our good old family tree.
> I just couldn't be the person they expected me to be
> And the biggest disappointment in the world was me.

My brother, Bobby, was my friend, and in contrast to me, he was successful in his pursuits and led a happy life. He loved fishing and hunting wild boar, only abandoning these pursuits years later when he became a staunch vegetarian.

From twelve years of age, my brother trained in karate and reached the level of black belt, third dan. He was also very interested in the aboriginal heritage of Australia, and after initially being given a didgeridoo as a gift, he developed a fine skill in playing and making didgeridoos. His 'talking didgeridoo' performances brought the aboriginal traditions to life.

Bobby had an inbuilt kindness and genuine acceptance and liking of people whatever their circumstances.

When I returned from hospital, Bobby had moved into a house with two of his mates—they nicknamed their new abode 'The Orphanage'.

It was no surprise that harmony would not come easily when I moved back home—but we tried. At the time, we used to liken ourselves to the characters from the television situation comedy *Fawlty Towers*, with my father as Basil, my mother as Sybil, and myself as Polly, the maid.

My Aunty Annie was nearby, and I was also able to visit her often. Her complete acceptance of me always made for an uplifting time.

Another outing that we all enjoyed was visiting my mother's friend Jean and her husband, Walter. We played the card game 500. There was a lot of friendly rivalry over this, and I especially remember the challenging fire in my father's eyes when he declared his favourite suite of 'misere'.

In her younger years, Jean had been a missionary in Egypt, and to my way of thinking, was a very practical Christian who had also been there for me when I came back from Hong Kong. I was only one of many to whom she extended a helping, but not pushy, hand.

I used to go for long walks with my father, and occasionally we would get up early on Sunday morning and walk to the local flea market.

For many years, the whole family had gone to my mother's church every Sunday, but now only my mother and Aunty Annie attended, after which Aunty Annie stayed for lunch. In return, once a month, Aunty Annie and I used to cook something special and sometimes experimental at 'Annie's Restaurant' located in her home.

Our most famous misadventure was a magnificent-looking devil's food cake, which we made as a special birthday cake for Jo, Daniel, and Aunty Annie—all three birthdays occurring within three days of each other. When the two sponges sank in the middles, we rescued their dismal appearance by filling the depressions with sweet butter cream icing, which maintained the cake's shape and splendid appearance. The thick wedges that everyone had chosen (except for the chefs) brought several requests for, 'A dry biscuit, please.' By an ironic twist of fate, we had chosen candles that perfectly complemented the cake, and there was no need to 'send in the clowns' to save the 'show', because they were already there.

Shortly after this, Daniel began having problems and returned to hospital. He absconded whilst on leave and went interstate. He used to ring Auntie Annie, who always took his reverse-charge calls, and left a lifeline open for him. During this time, Daniel's behaviour seemed completely out of character, and when he finally returned, we parted company soon after.

We did keep in touch over the years with occasional meetings and letters until his very sad demise nine years later. He was a very dear man.

Chapter 23

Once a week, on Sunday night, I was allowed to take the car to attend the little Welsh church with Jo, who lived just across the road from it.

Occasionally I could drive to see Jo and Tania during the week. Other times, I used to walk over, with the neighbour's dog, Snoopy, who ran all the way. Regardless of his small stature, he tackled any other canines who crossed his track. I had gained these new freedoms after a 'family discussion'.

It was on one of these visits that I met a man who was to have a very positive influence in my life for many years to come. This was Vincent, whom Jo described as a successful businessman. He was also the owner of a horse property, part of which bordered along the back fence of Jo's place. He and his wife, Ruth, lived about mile from the property.

Life seemed to be settling into a tolerable state with some happy days and a supportive network growing around me. It was November 1988. Jo and Tania were going on a two-week holiday to Sydney, and they asked me if I would like to house sit for them while they were away and feed their cat, Tiddles. They had no one else to turn to, and although I wasn't overly fond of cats, I liked the whole idea of some time on my own. My parents agreed reluctantly, but when it came right down to it, they didn't give me a moment's peace whilst I was there. They were on the phone, ringing me up all the time wanting to know what I was doing and asking if they could come round.

Truth to tell, most of the time I was cleaning. The little house was full of ornaments and shelves, with little nooks and crannies that had hardly seen the light of day, and I thought I would surprise my friends when they came back.

As usual, sleeping in a strange place posed a problem. I had hoped that this wouldn't happen as I was very familiar with the house and had spent many happy hours there previously, just chatting, drinking coffee, and smoking in the friendly environment. I used to think this was much more therapeutic and beneficial than all the hours spent with doctors and in 'treatment' in hospital.

When I couldn't sleep, I'd take another lithium tablet, hoping this would be helpful, although I'd never had much success with this method before. In fact, this could have been the most problematic course of action I could have taken.

I recall the night before this next unanticipated event, a week after I came to stay. The bed felt smooth and comforting as I lay down that evening, but sleep would not come, and the shapes in the darkened room were unfamiliar. Shadows from the trees outside moved across the window in a pattern I did not recognize.

I challenged the darkness to let me find peace—concentrated my thoughts on lying still, and then I must have drifted off, but into one of those light sleeps when you feel you are still awake.

The morning brought with it refreshing light, and I took advantage of the sunshine to do my washing and let it dry quickly. I was tired but happy and listening to my favourite tape, *His Hand in Mine* by Elvis Presley.

Late that afternoon, I went and sat under the tree near the fence and watched the horses grazing. I had been sitting there for about an hour when I felt that something was wrong. I don't know why, but I started feeling the ground all around me, near the tree's roots. I had a sense of foreboding, but told myself I was being silly. However, I continued feeling all around. I had felt about three quarters of the way around the tree, and had found nothing—whatever 'it' might be.

I made myself walk around to the place I hadn't yet felt, just to make sure. Then, to my shock, as I felt further, I felt the top of something buried in the dirt—and straight away, I 'knew'. I believed it was something that had been planted there, and it would contaminate the whole area.

I had not seen what it looked like at that time, but I had to get it out of there. I dug it out with my hands. It was a rectangular shape, about ten inches by four inches, and six inches deep, black and heavy, and it started making a noise like a muffled whisper.

I believed I must take it 'far away and in a straight line'. Why I thought that, I didn't know, but I felt compelled to do it. I walked with it across the road, and kept walking till I sat down not far from the railway track, way past the little Welsh church.

A man came along with his dog, and because I knew I was looking upset, and couldn't tell him the real reason, I told him I had two bowling balls in the box, and I was sad because I'd had an argument with the person who'd given them to me.

They kept on walking and went by.

It was starting to get dark then, but I had resigned myself that I had to keep going—where to, I didn't know. I was convinced I couldn't just leave 'it' and go back, although I wanted to.

It was making the noise again, and I told it, 'Shut up!' many times.

It seemed to me that I had to undergo a series of 'tests' before I would be freed of the 'thing'.

I had no shoes; there were prickles everywhere, but I just kept on moving through fences and whatever came along, still carrying the 'thing', still walking in a straight line. I had scratches all over me as I had fallen over many times, but I still kept on going, carrying this heavy box.

It had become dark, and the night had taken on a 'world' or 'life' of its own.

At one time, a group of horses, real or imagined or conjured up, ran all around me in a circle, whinnying and carrying on. Another time, I looked up at a tree and was startled to see what looked like a very large image of a man's head and the top half of his body, looking down at me—the shape and shadows of the tree gave this impression, and I recognized this at the time.

And all this time, I kept telling this 'thing'—this 'box'—that I knew that none of it was real. I thought it was like 'magic' making illusions from the surroundings.

I walked through some soft manure, but frightened myself by thinking it was a dead cat I was stepping on. At one time, I smacked my head down on the ground because that was another 'test'.

Just after that, there were some lights, and the surroundings started to look a bit familiar. In spite of my 'pledge' to walk in a straight line only, I realized I was not far from the little shop just up the road from Jo and Tania's house. I must have gone in a large semi-circle.

I had fallen down again, and was searching in the long grass for the 'thing', but I couldn't find it.

Then I smelt this strange smell. I could see nothing, but I really believed some unseen force had been playing tricks on me. I cursed the night to hell and offered every insult I could think of and ran down the street back to the sanctuary of Jo's house.

After my apparently-self-imposed ordeal, I found I had finally 'freed myself and miraculously returned home'. I then had to contemplate the stinging cuts and bruises I had all over me. I found some disinfectant and applied it to my legs, which were the most affected, and I was rewarded with an even more painful result. But I was glad to be home!

I couldn't believe the night's events, which I relived over and over in my mind. Questions kept firing at me: Was the whole episode real and based on some sort of hidden facts, or logic, or was it pure imagination? Were there really evil forces out there who had placed me in some form of entrancement, or was I so tired I was living a dream?'

How could I tell anyone about this? I didn't think I could.

I mentioned it to Vincent, and he tried to laugh it off, but I could see it made him uneasy.

Obviously, no one was going to take this seriously, so in order to explain my injuries, I never mentioned a word except to say that I had fallen down some stairs.

> High today. Looks a mess—will need admission. Agrees to come voluntarily. Admit. (FOI)

This was just a short stay, but the events that preceded it gave me more anguish than I could ever have anticipated. This was another of the bizarre events I couldn't explain at the time, which convinced me more than ever that I must really have manic depression.

It is somewhat ironic that the 'bizarre events' were what persuaded me that I must be suffering from manic depression, and yet my doctors knew none of these details.

My readers may think that, after such an adventure into 'unreality', there was no hope for me at all. However, the greatest opportunities were to open up to me after this most unlikely of events.

PART 3

Victory over the Consequences

Chapter 24

The day had dawned sunny with clear skies, but there was a sweetness in the air that hadn't been there before.

I had always believed that living at home and listening to constant recriminations and negative expectations of my goals or future aspirations affected me so much that it virtually pushed me over the edge. I had pleaded my case to my brother when he had come to visit me prior to my discharge from hospital. He was about to embark on an adventure holiday to northern Queensland, and pledged that, on his return, I could come and stay with him and his future wife, Karen. He was as good as his word, and there I was, waking up in a friendly environment to new beginnings.

Coincidentally, confirmation had arrived that my application to pursue a bachelor of arts at the University of Queensland, St Lucia campus, had been accepted. It was also during this time that I heard the theory relating to the genetic cause of manic depression, as outlined in the introduction to this book, and for the first time, I felt able to accept this explanation and truly move forwards.

Bobby had opened a door of opportunity that I had proven over and over again, I was unable to do on my own. I have no doubt at all that, without his intervention, there would have been no 'Victory over the Consequences' to relate in this book.

This was a very big turning point, and it acted as a springboard for my future success. It seemed that no obstacle was too big for my brother, and he went to bat for me. Firstly, he encouraged our parents to support me in my quest to study at university. For three months, Karen lent me her car so I could travel to and from my classes. My parents were considering buying a new car, and Bobby persuaded them to give me their old one when they had another car. How he did it, I don't know, but he always did have more influence over them than I had.

I was very grateful to Bobby and Karen, and my life assumed a new harmony and fell into a pleasing rhythm. The turnaround in all aspects of my life was amazing . . . almost unbelievable.

Three weeks after I moved in with Bobby and Karen and gained my newfound independence, Dr Sorensen described me as 'very well presented and realistic' (FOI Notes). He also reduced my lithium intake to six tablets a day—this was two tablets fewer than I had been on prior to this move.

Dr Sorensen took a keen interest in my university studies, and as time went by, I began to feel more like a colleague than a patient. He was very encouraging and listened to my plans and goals with interest.

After four months, I gave up smoking. After six months, I moved out into a flat of my own. Every Friday night, I called in to visit my parents.

My friend Jo sold her little house and moved down to Coff's Harbour to be close to her niece and family, but I maintained my friendship with Vincent, whom I had met there a year previously. Vincent's passion was the classic Arabian horse, and I began visiting his horse stud to help out with the more mundane chores such as shovelling manure out of the stables. Over the following years, I learnt a great deal about every aspect of the care of horses, and came to appreciate their beauty. I especially liked the way they were true to their own character and didn't present different faces and personalities the way many people do.

For some reason, Vincent always believed in me and my ability, and was my true friend and confidant for thirteen of the best and happiest years of my life.

He used to say that, whatever happened, 'take it in your stride', and I have never forgotten those wise words.

As I began to feel more secure in my new life, my long struggle to live my life in the way I wanted seemed to fade in my mind. Each day seemed full of opportunity, with a peacefulness and a surety I had never felt before.

I soon switched from monthly visits to Dr Sorensen to every-other-month visits and then every-four-month visits. They no longer seemed threats or battles to be won, but more like affirmations that everything was going well.

All of my relationships were positive at this time, and my parents came to accept my new lifestyle.

Initially, I was studying social work, but after six months, I changed to a bachelor of arts with a double major in psychology, because I believed I had an understanding of life situations that could benefit others.

I liked attending university. It was exciting and alive, made so by the students and lecturers from diverse backgrounds, cultures, dress style, and age.

When I entered university, I was thirty-five years of age, but I did not feel out of place at all. The constantly moving tide of students travelling from one lecture and location to another embraced me, and I felt safe, secure, adventurous, and triumphant!

My FOI notes reflect the dramatic change that had taken place in my life. Short positive entries from my visits with Dr Sorensen:

> Work—good
> Sleep—good
> Studies—good
> Family—good
> Friendships—good

On only two occasions was there an entry: 'speaking a little rapid, but okay.'

My serum lithium results remained constant, and I was not taking any other medication.

I was always aware that lack of sleep had been causative to my previous problems. However, the time I spent with the horses, shovelling out stables, carrying water buckets, wheeling barrows of food, and unloading hay and chaff, generally made me tired enough that sleep was not a problem.

Happily, I had also discovered that, on the occasional times I could not drift into sleep easily, I would fall asleep if I took two soluble aspirins and lay still.

Sometimes, I would break my own rule and spend a whole night completing an assignment, but as I did this only occasionally, it did not prove problematic.

The most painful event happened when I was working with Vincent and his horses. 'That hurt!' I winced as I cradled my left hand. It was early evening, and light was fading, the only time I could call in to help with the serving of the mare.

I had led the mare into the arena and climbed over the fence, still holding the lead rope. Then I had talked to her and soothed her as Vincent brought the stallion in. The stallion, in his eagerness, jumped on the mare sideways causing her to buck and kick in her distress. Vincent and I had pre-arranged that, in the event of any danger in the servicing, I was to drop the lead rope. I attempted to do this, but, at the same time, the mare moved forwards crushing my hand against the fence post. She then raised her head, and the rope burnt through my trapped hand. Even then, I did not know how badly my hand was injured, but because it was important to the breeding programme, the mare had to stand for a second time. I held the lead rope in my other hand, and all went smoothly on the second attempt.

Only after we had returned to the lit stable block did it become obvious that I would need to go straight up to the emergency department at Ipswich General Hospital

With my hand healing, I continued my studies and took another gigantic step forward. It was then that I moved into a flat of my own, and left behind the sanctuary Bobby and Karen had provided for me.

Chapter 25

The large pipe organ roared into life as the academics in various regalia took their places on the podium. This was followed by an introductory and congratulatory speech from the university chancellor before the graduates came forward, one after the other, to receive their graduation scroll, proclaiming their bachelor of arts degree.

Cameras flashed, and excitement filled the air! It was a sweltering day, but it was pride that flushed my features as reflected in the photos taken later that day with my mother, father, Bobby, and Auntie Annie. It was a happy day for my family, and I did feel truly victorious!

Although I had achieved my bachelor of arts, I needed a higher score in two of my subjects to be eligible to complete my master's degree. This was necessary to practice as a psychologist. I opted to do these two subjects over the next year. Although I succeeded in the upgrading, I still remained a couple of percentage points below the entrance level required for that year. Philosophically, I accepted this and vowed to find an opportunity to use my degree in a different way, but in a way that would still be beneficial for other people.

During this year, my parents had moved into a new unit that was smaller and more manageable than our large family house had been. I often used to call in on my way home, and our relationship was the best it had ever been. There were also those days when I dropped in on the spur of the moment, only to find my father had already been expecting me. We seemed to be on the same wavelength.

Since leaving home five years previously, I had been taking six lithium tablets a day with no incidents at all. In June 1993, I discussed this with Dr Sorensen, and he agreed to lower my dosage to four tablets a day. I was elated by this, feeling I was now taking a positive and proactive part in my treatment. As you may recall, this relaxed conversation was outlined in the introduction. My father was equally delighted about this, and life was good!

Then, four months later, I received an early morning phone call from my father: 'We've both cracked up!' were his cryptic words. I went straight over to see them. They half joked that it must have been the pies they had eaten in a recent pie drive they had supported. Nevertheless, Mother was well again within a week, but Father's illness lingered. Although suffering from late-onset diabetes and, for the previous year, from Parkinson's disease, he had remained as active as possible, going for long walks with his friends.

He was very appreciative of the care my mother had given him as his illness progressed and told her that she was a good girl for looking after him so well. This made her smile because he was not a man given to false praise.

He had always been very proud of his two grandchildren, Erin and Harry, and had always found energy to play with them, hide-and-seek being their favourite game. They fondly called him Pa Pa.

My brother and I called in nearly every day during this period of ill health. Father had a series of diagnostic tests, after which Dr Johnson recommended a short stay in hospital to help with his recovery.

It was early evening, still and hot, and I was feeding the horses with Vincent. On glancing up, I noticed Bobby approaching. By his demeanour and downcast gaze, I knew something was wrong. Even then, I could never have anticipated his words which made my heart sink: 'Pa Pa had a heart attack tonight—they tried to revive him and he came back—but then he died of kidney failure.'

These words echoed over and over in my mind. It seemed unreal. Only a few hours before, he had walked into hospital unaided with Mother and me. He had obviously been unwell, but had still managed to make us smile. As he had lain on the narrow hospital bed in his street clothes, I had taken off his sandals for him, kissed him goodbye, and told him I would be back the next morning.

Bobby and Mother had gone to visit him that evening, at the time of his heart attack, and Bobby had been with him as the hospital team strove to stabilize him. 'What are they doing to you?' he'd asked our father.

Father replied in a joking way, 'Everything!'

As it unfolded, Douglas Murray Oliver, who had been so relentless in life, showed courage in the face of death and eternity.

He had demonstrated determination and persistence, and always remained true to what he believed. He was kind hearted to those who knew him well, and he had the strength of his own integrity.

To me, he was inspirational in the face of all the upset my search for the truth had caused, and he never lost faith in any member of his family. Like a true diamond, he had inner strength and not just sparkle. His life had spanned seventy-four years.

Chapter 26

The night of my father's death was the saddest night of my life. I was very upset, but determined that I would speak at his funeral as a final tribute, and that night I completed the eulogy. Sleep came slowly and restlessly.

But life went on, and the funeral was organized.

The night before the funeral, I decided to put a photo of my father in the locket I wore around my neck. Sitting on my bed, I carefully cut out the photo and placed it in the locket. Then I placed the small silver frame around it securely and snapped the locket tightly closed.

The next morning, I was walking through the lounge room into the kitchen to have some breakfast. As I did so, I noticed something glinting on the floor. I bent down to look at it and was amazed to find it was the small silver frame I had placed in the locket the night before. The locket was still closed securely. How had that frame gotten there? I took this as a sign that my father was still with me, and this made me feel happy and enabled me to deliver his eulogy in a very positive manner.

After the funeral, my cousin Liz and I followed the hearse to the crematorium. When we arrived, the driver had waited for us, and, in a very moving and understanding way, gave me two carnations from the top of the coffin.

We parked the car alongside several others, and walked around the grounds for a little while, and then prepared to return home. When Liz began to back the car out, it stalled. She started it again, and immediately it stalled again. At the same moment, another car passed behind us. If our car had kept going, we would have collided. Liz could not understand why the engine had failed twice, as it was a brand new car and it had never happened before

I felt my father was protecting us.

Liz stayed with me for several days. We talked about all sorts of related matters from within her own experience—of people dying and still seeming to be present.

Before the strange events happened, I had been coping quite well with my father's passing, but after them I clung to the desperate hope that somehow he was still with me.

Sleep became very difficult. Even when Liz had been there, it had been very spasmodic, my thoughts turning over and over these unexpected occurrences. In addition, I kept looking for more 'signs'.

After she left, I knew it was dangerous for me to go without sleep for too long. I tried the soluble aspirin, and I took extra lithium, and sleep finally came.

But when it did, it brought with it a disturbing dream that was so vivid it made me wonder if it had really happened. Like so many dreams, it was a mix of familiar places and unlikely events. It took place deep in a coal mine, somewhere near the Welsh church. In my dream, charges were being set to destroy an evil force.

The Welsh church is just across the road from where the horses were, and I had come home after the evening feed that night before I had this dream. There are old coalmines in this general area, but I did not know anything of their history.

When I awoke, it was the middle of the night, and I kept thinking about this dream.

The house I lived in had enough mystery of its own—it was an old house that had been the manor house on the estate. It was still very large, even though part of it had been separated and moved to another location.

The young couple in the flat next to mine had, weeks previously, come to me very upset. They said they were leaving because of a disturbing series of events. Their bathroom door had slammed shut one night, and on entering to investigate, they felt a cold breeze and smelt an unfamiliar perfume. This had apparently happened more than once. The incident that had made their decision to leave so imperative had also occurred at night. A framed picture on the wall had fallen down whilst they were sleeping. They had been startled awake, and were shocked to find the picture lodged, inexplicably, upside down behind the mirror on the bedroom dresser. This defied all logic, and they asked me if I had had any similar experiences.

My lounge room was certainly very interesting, as I had discovered. The walls were very high, and to the casual observer, looked of equal height, but they were all different—only strategically placed curtain rods and borders gave the appearance of symmetry.

My own experiences were limited to the curtains moving in my bedroom when all the doors and windows were closed. However, I had been told that there were probably ventilation shafts in this large house, which could explain why the curtains moved. Nonetheless, I sometimes had to convince myself that there was nothing more sinister when I closed my eyes to sleep.

So I lay there, reliving this dream for maybe half an hour. Then, without warning, there was a tinkling crash from the direction of the kitchen. I had an ornamental mobile hanging there, and amongst other things, it had little bells hanging from it. I thought this must have fallen down, and after the initial shock, I tentatively went to check it out. Nothing had fallen. I laughed and thought this must be another sign from my father.

But there was an eeriness that made me feel uncomfortable, and I started to believe the dream could be true. Maybe there was a war against evil going on. I lay down on my bed again and vowed to wait out the night and get out of there in the morning.

I then drifted into another uneasy sleep, which brought with it another vivid and disturbing dream. This time, I dreamt I was at home, packing for a journey and waiting for my companion traveller—but I was fearful in my dream that I was not safe while I waited. I woke up feeling scared, but safe at the same time, when I realized it was only a dream.

I put on the light before going to the kitchen to have a cold drink. When I returned to my bedroom, I left the light on and reflected on my two vivid dreams and the 'nonexistent' crashing sound from the kitchen. What did it all mean? Did it mean anything? Was my father still with me, or was I just all confused due to wishful thinking?

I felt better with the light on. I'd had some kind of rest, and I was relatively calm.

What now? I thought. *Maybe there's something in this house that is causing me to have these dreams.* As well, I had no real explanation for the tinkling crash in the kitchen. If it had been a sign from my father, it certainly wasn't a very comforting or reassuring one.

And so I began a search, looking for anything that might have some association with evil. The house was in disarray by morning. I hadn't found anything of any real significance, but the house looked as if it had been ransacked.

I decided to abandon this search, and go back to my original idea of getting out of there and catching a train to Brisbane.

This wasn't going to be something I was going to be able to explain very easily.

In spite of everything, I thought I was still rational, and as I walked slowly to the railway station, I really believed that the house was a battleground for evil. I didn't know what I would find when I returned.

As I sat at the railway station, I did not know what to make of the night's events, but I knew they definitely fitted the category of the bizarre—something I would have to keep to myself.

My father's death had been overshadowed. I had believed he was still with me in spirit, but this was no longer a comfort.

By then it was mid-morning. I had only loose change, but enough for a return ticket. I needed to take some time to try and work this out. I arrived at Central Station, sat on platform bench, and watched the myriad of people coming and going as I continued my inward reflection. Eventually, I boarded a train and returned from whence I'd come. I had decided to say the house had been broken into, but my reasoning was starting to lose its focus.

I remember walking through the train and seeing a group made up of two young men and their girlfriends. One of these men had blonde hair, was very loud, and seemed very pleased with himself. I thought he was very effeminate and gave him a pink ribbon to put in his hair. He looked amazed when I gave it to him.

The trip seemed endless, but finally I alighted at my station and trudged wearily homewards. The house was open, just as I had left it, and in the afternoon sunlight, it looked chaotic but innocuous.

I started to tidy up a little, and became fascinated with a booklet on Monet, which I had studied at university. Because the book was upside down, I developed the 'concept' that for some unrevealed reason, everything had to be upside down and back to front.

Bobby called in, and in view of the state of the house and my demeanour, he invited me to stay the night with him and his family. However, I was no sooner left alone in my room, than I walked quietly downstairs and began arranging some itemised bottles of nails and screws on the workbench, into an upside down and back to front pattern. I then carried some of these bottles through the open roller door of the garage and placed them in the box trailer attached to the back of Bobby's Toyota Hilux that was parked outside the house.

I subsequently agreed to his suggestion that I should go to the psyche hospital. The lengthy procedure of being admitted meant that, once again, I found no relief in sleep, and my medical examination revealed that I was wearing my bra back to front, and I was convinced that the clock was going backwards.

I offered no explanation for my dress sense, and I remember their knowing look when I told them I had spent the day on a train. Although this was true, they did record in my medical notes that I seemed unconcerned that someone had 'broken in to my house and left it looking trashed'. (FOI Notes)

Chapter 27

So, once again, I was going voluntarily to hospital for treatment after another bizarre incident. Once again, I was going to be treated when the doctors knew none of the details of what had really happened. I was also certain that, if I told them the truth, I might never walk free again!

The main difference with this admission was that, even though nobody could understand my actions, they believed my behaviour had been caused by the sudden death of my father.

In reality, this was the precursor behind the real reason—my poor sleeping pattern.

This was to be my last admission to hospital—seventeen years ago—and the first time I felt fully supported, with no anger directed towards me on account of my actions.

This hospitalization comprised much the same variety of treatment and response as my stay five years previously, but with some interesting variations. The most noteworthy difference was my blood pressure; on admission it was 200/130 (FOI Notes) So much emphasis was put on the cause of this and trying to lower the reading that it assumed a high priority. Notwithstanding that my own general practitioner had documented my 'white collar hypertension', a condition I shared with my father. Dr Johnson confirmed this condition to my hospital doctors during my treatment.

A litany of tests including an electro-encephalogram and twenty-four-hour urine collection confirmed that I had come to the hospital free of any 'recreational drugs'. (FOI Notes)

When I entered hospital, I was behaving strangely, following a theme of 'upside-down and back to front', and my sleep had been spasmodic.

It was two days after admission before I fell into a drug-induced sleep. After that, my focus was centred on 'surviving the treatment'. Before I left, my lithium was increased until it reached the toxic level of 1.4 before it was ceased for approximately two weeks, and then resumed at four tablets a day.

I was once again plagued by serious side effects as the drug-intensive therapy progressed. I went through the whole gamut of emotions:

happiness on my birthday when my mother brought me a cake, happiness to be supported by my family, frustration by the effects of treatment, anger that caused me to abuse a doctor and staff, regret when I apologized, fear of falling down any flight of steps I had to walk down; complete disorientation to where my bed was or what I was doing. On top of these emotions, I was unable to dress myself properly, I urinated on the floor, and I suffered from restless legs.

I swayed from one extreme to the other, but overall, everyone was working towards a resolution of these symptoms, and a happy recovery. Over the six-week period, I began to inch my way forwards. I was granted day leave, then weekend leave, and finally I was discharged. But not before the attempt was made to introduce me to another drug, clonazepam. I had been given it twice as per the admitting doctor's instruction, but after that, Dr Sorensen had allowed me the option—and the privilege—of refusing this additional medication. After two weeks of my adamant refusal, this drug was withdrawn.

Finally I returned to the life I had left behind and continued working with the horses. Two months later, I resumed study at the Queensland University of Technology (QUT) and successfully completed my graduate diploma in education that year. I was then a qualified and registered teacher in early childhood (from birth to eight years).

But the thought still lingered, *Am I always going to be a victim of these 'bizarre events'?*

Chapter 28

Poignant sadness were the words I recorded on the day of Daniel's funeral. This farewell was tinged with irreconcilable sorrow as his final battle for survival had ended in his brave suicide.

The pastor's words stayed with me, 'When the sky is blackest, the stars are brightest.'

I journeyed in my thoughts to days gone by—to the day we had walked out of hospital as defiant absconders . . . picnics every Saturday . . . visits at home when I was studying for my senior. A myriad of thoughts came back to me.

I looked at his photo over and over, and read the words he had written on the back: 'Here's me looking at you and all your charms.' I read his letters, and my heart was wrenched—but life went on. It had been nine years since we had parted company.

A year later, I had a visit from a mutual friend, Jo, and we remembered him anew.

On the following day, there it was on the dull-green, carpeted floor, its glistening lustre compelling me to notice it. I knew straight away that the pearl I was staring at was the one I had kept for almost a decade after it had found its way loose from the ring Daniel had given me. It was a real mystery to me how it had suddenly 'appeared', as I had not looked at it for quite a while. *How did it get here? Is he still with me?*

I started again down that path that would have led to restless nights . . . the path that would have led me to believe that Daniel was still with me, but underlying that, that there was evil lurking . . . lurking wherever my thoughts would take me. It wasn't hard to imagine faces at the night window trying to get in. It wasn't hard to believe I was under some invisible form of attack though safely secure in my familiar unit.

The summer heat was oppressive, and even the whirring of the overhead fan sounded menacing. I could have continued down that track, but this time, in the midst of what could have become another bizarre incident, the cold, hard, clear voice of logic took over. I said to myself, *Stop! Stop thinking like this. No matter how real it seems to be, you know it's not real. Nothing will happen if you disregard these thoughts you are thinking. Nothing will happen—you are creating this fear yourself.*

For the first time, I was able to logically override the fear and insecurities that were ready to take over in the midst of memories and loss.

I went back to bed feeling peaceful, and miraculously slept till morning. I took that day off work and regained my perspective.

That weekend, I attended a horse show, and by Monday I was back at work refreshed, moving forwards, and feeling 'truly victorious'.

This to me was the turning point—knowing that I could reverse a potential bizarre event. I could reverse it by my thinking, building upon my previous experiences, and extending my previous conclusions. This gave me a power I had not had before, and this realization brought with it the relief I had long been searching for.

And strangely enough, I have never had another bizarre experience or the potential for the same, in all of the many years since.

Chapter 29

At the same time, life was leading me down a different pathway. Since my father's demise, I had become firmly established in my career path as a director in childcare. My duties included general administration, working as a pre-school teacher or group leader as necessary, covering lunch relief, attending lectures and workshops with staff, and assisting them with their studies. I was also responsible for supervising room programming, leading accreditation preparation, and presiding over monthly staff and parent meetings. Additionally, I enjoyed organising social events and fundraising and promotional activities, which involved a great deal of involvement with parents and staff. I worked closely with children from all backgrounds including those with disabilities—the centres were always happy and welcoming for children and their parents. I threw myself wholeheartedly into my career.

My previous habit of monthly hospital visits had long ceased, and I attended only when I needed a new prescription.

My life was changing in other ways also. After thirteen years, I stopped working with the horses, and parted company with Vincent, who had been my mentor and greatest inspiration over that period.

In September 2000, my landlord for the previous six years became my neighbour in the unit next to mine, and our friendship turned to romance. Thus began my journey with the man I was to marry and walk beside for the remaining adventures in my life. I had been with Benjamin for a full year before I mentioned anything about my previous experiences in hospital and my diagnosis of manic depression. I felt quite downcast at this confession, but it did not seem to faze Benjamin, who had spent four years as a psychiatric nurse in Wales in the United Kingdom.

My mother became very fond of Benjamin, and to my way of thinking, this was a welcome and refreshing response. She accepted him and trusted him, and he was very open with her, and very attentive to her needs when she became unwell. Benjamin became part of our family, and when my mother passed away a year later, I believe she felt a little more at peace that I was finally with someone whom she liked and respected.

During the time I had been with Benjamin, I had begun putting on weight, and decided to try and arrest this pattern. I visited a local naturopath who put me on a programme of weight reduction. I knew that lithium encouraged weight gain through the retention of fluid, so I decided to risk halving my dose of lithium. This took me down to two 250 mg tablets per day. I lost the desired weight, and my health remained at its optimum.

When I next saw Dr Sorensen, I confirmed I had been taking the lower amount, and he continued my prescription at this lower rate. From 2001, I obtained my prescriptions from my local general practitioner and never visited a psychiatrist again.

For eight years, I maintained this level of lithium, too low to be of any therapeutic value, but ready to be built up if needed. I had one serum lithium test done in 2008, with a reading of 0.3.

And life went on—I continued working as a child care director with no incidents of any kind requiring additional treatment or hospitalization.

Writing this book gave me a perspective I couldn't achieve when I was in the midst of the situation, in real time. From studying my own words that I had written at the time, combined with the detail in my Freedom of Information notes, it became clear to me that high doses and overdoses of lithium preceded the events that I could neither explain nor understand—those that I termed bizarre.

These events had only occurred after 1978 when I had first accepted my diagnosis. Lack of sleep caused by unfamiliar surroundings or by constant reflection and over-thinking had been exacerbated when I took extra lithium in the belief that it would offer salvation and could induce sleep.

I saw this pattern repeated over and over in the dysfunctional periods of my life, when I could offer no explanation for my actions, yet retained the clear memory of my distorted thinking.

Then, in 2009, I consulted *Guide to Drugs and Supplements* published two years previously by Readers Digest Australia. Listed amongst the myriad of possible side effects of lithium were hallucinations. Listed amongst the overdose symptoms were bizarre thoughts or hallucinations.

So there it was, a recognized link between the medication being causative to the symptoms it was prescribed to alleviate. I could hardly believe it. This offered an explanation I had never considered, but it was certainly supported by my own experiences.

I was already aware of the possible serious side effects of the other medications I had been on, but this revelation about lithium really set me thinking.

And so convinced was I that lithium was no salvation—just a health risk to my kidneys and thyroid gland as the years progressed—in combination with the fact that, for the last seventeen years, I had had no issues requiring treatment or hospitalization, I decided to go down to one table a day for six weeks and observe if there were any undesirable effects. This was a difficult and scary decision, after all my previous history, and it made my pulse race to think about it, but it also seemed inevitable.

I remembered my father's oft repeated saying, 'A man convinced against his will is of the same opinion still.' I felt more than ever, that I was that 'man' and this was my time to act on my belief, or alternatively wonder for the rest of my life if I could have lived without fear and without lithium!

Chapter 30

So I took the plunge.

After six weeks of taking one tablet of lithium per day, I completely stopped taking it. From 4 May 2009, I was no longer on lithium!

As it transpired, this was a very tumultuous period of my life, but I reminded myself that, in the past, lithium had not improved my response to life situations, so I reasoned I was no worse off without it.

It seemed like the kaleidoscope of my life was once again turning and that I was lost somewhere in the midst of it all, trying to maintain equilibrium.

My administrative tasks as a childcare director sometimes became very demanding. I had a great team, and by the beginning of July that year, we had successfully gone through the annual audit and the annual general meeting, and we had put in the final application for the staff's new enterprise bargaining agreement. We were in a good position to move forwards.

I had been pushing myself along to achieve these results, and had arranged to have a week's leave. Though this seemed sensible and well accepted at the time, information I learnt during this time precipitated a series of events that had a domino effect in my life. Just prior to this scheduled week away from work, I learned from a mutual friend that my previous mentor and friend, Vincent, had suffered a medical condition two years previously that had left him seriously physically incapacitated. This hit me hard and caused me a lot of distress, even though I had been out of contact with Vincent for ten years.

Benjamin and I visited Vincent and his wife, and he assured us that, although he had been through some very tough times, he was managing well. He told us this with an appreciative smile towards Ruth. Indeed, his quick wit and sense of humour seemed remarkably intact.

Then on 4 August, during the chilling winter months, my thoughts were once again centred on this whole situation, and I found that my breathing was becoming more and more difficult. I thought I was going to die, and was wailing this out in an agonizing way between each laboured breath.

Ben called the ambulance. They arrived and administered oxygen. I stumbled, but was able to walk with support downstairs, and was then stretchered into the ambulance. By the time we reached the local hospital, I was responding well, and began breathing normally and unaided. A cardiogram revealed there seemed to be nothing wrong, and at half past eleven that night, I was allowed to return home.

However, questions asked by the attending doctor whilst I was at the hospital sent my thoughts and logic in another direction. It had been three months since my monthly periods had ceased abruptly. Although in my mid-fifties, I had taken a pregnancy test, which had shown a negative result. I had quite happily accepted this result at the time, paying little attention to the wording, 'If you are of menopausal age, you might get a false reading.' On reflection, I remembered my extreme tiredness and increased appetite of the past few months, and began to believe I might be pregnant. As though by magic, my body began to display more and more characteristics typical of pregnancy, and my body shape and weight all supported my growing belief. An early ultrasound had been negative, but a later doppler ultrasound gave an unmistakeable positive result and foetal heartbeat—this was truly remarkable—but this also turned out to be false!

So, after a ride on elation, tinged with anxiety about the whole situation, and then eventual sadness, I had to turn my thinking around and began a major fitness and weight-loss program.

I had left work and was at one of my lowest ebbs. I now had to do some serious regrouping, but in spite of everything, I did not restart taking lithium.

Whether this whole event was a manic episode, a menopausal episode, or a profound reaction to ceasing lithium, I don't know.

Benjamin and I rode out these events and remained strong together. I had been off work for six months.

My fitness plan was in place, and I continued to lose weight and gain fitness after once again resuming work as a director in childcare. This time, my centre was close to home, so I gained the two and a half hours that used to be my travelling time. This gave me more time for relaxation.

So here it is now, in current time—January 2011. I have been back at work for twelve months, and it's been eighteen months since I stopped taking lithium. I am still feeling confident and optimistic. I have resumed my goal of moving overseas to live permanently in Wales with Benjamin, who is now my husband.

I am convinced that my life can continue happily without the need for lithium or any other psychiatric drug.

AFTERWORD

Unravelling the Mystery

Unravelling the Mystery

Looking back may hold the key
That allows you to move forwards,
To see beyond that keyhole of despair
And unlock you from the prison of deep fear.

So what were the odds I was up against?
What was my genetic past?
Where were the cryptic clues leading?
Why was my father expecting my diagnosis of manic depression?

My Freedom of Information Notes revealed a genetic past strongly linked to depression, hospitalization, and one recorded incidence of melancholia. One great-uncle had lived most of his life in a mental institution and finally died there. These were on my mother's side.

My maternal grandmother had suffered recurrent breakdowns and depression. My own research into my heritage confirmed she had died of cardiac failure due to encephalitis after a two-week stay in the district hospital at Wangarratta when she was just thirty-nine years old. My mother had suffered with depression from the age of eighteen. (FOI Notes). Her three hospital admissions after she moved to Queensland, which included the administration of shock treatment, were all due to this condition.

On my father's side, depression and suicide were prevalent features, going back to my great-great-grandmother and great-great-grandfather, who both committed suicide by hanging, three months apart during 1856 in Scotland. This was confirmed by heritage research done by the Scottish Roots Ancestral Research Service based in Edinburgh. My great-grandfather committed suicide, also by hanging, two years after emigrating with his family to Australia. (FOI Notes)

My grandfather suffered depression in his later life after retirement. At the age of sixty-six years, he suffered a fatal coronary occlusion. This was on the day of his admission to Goodna Mental Hospital, which was one of the previous names for Wolston Park Hospital. (FOI Notes)

My father also kept some details of his own life well hidden. I had always known that he had had aspirations to be a lawyer, but I was unaware that after his scholarship year at a private grammar school, when his parents had been unable to afford to continue his tuition, he had gone through a period of serious depression at the age of sixteen years. My mother had shared this information with Bobby, who mentioned it to me after my father's passing.

This was certainly a formidable background.

I had known very little of this family history. Maybe if I had, I would have found it easier to accept my initial diagnosis of manic-depressive psychosis. Maybe!

I had always wondered about my mother's curious remark: 'Something happened to me, once, that was so bad, I'll never tell anyone. I'll take it to the grave with me.' She may have revealed the reason for this to my brother's wife, Karen. In the midst of an apparently unrelated conversation, something triggered a painful response from my mother, in which she revealed that her father had sexually abused her.

This admission verbalized the agonizing my mother must have endured over her long life. The shocking reality was that she had been let down completely by the one person she should have been able to rely on and trust, and yet she maintained a silence and loyalty over many decades. This struggle would certainly explain why my mother was so distrustful of men generally.

Only when she was eighty-three years of age did my mother confirm to me that this had happened to her. Surely it was a secret too painful to have carried alone for so long! No doubt the whole fabric of her life had been destroyed.

It may well be that her deep involvement with religion was a quest to learn how to forgive and still maintain her own integrity, faith, and values. Her own infidelity must have added to her burden, leaving her even more confused and let down. This may also explain why her standards for me seemed so harsh and unrelenting.

Her further comment, 'When the ambulance came, I thought it was a hearse. I thought I was dead. I wished I was dead,' may have been connected to her father's actions, or may have been a memory from any of the occasions she had suffered depression since her late teens. What it clearly shows is the intensity of her suffering. Her own mother passed away when she was only twelve years of age, leaving her to care for three younger siblings. This must have placed an incredible amount of responsibility on her young shoulders. It also meant that she had no mother to guide her through adolescence, and no role model to emulate when bringing up her own children.

In my father's attempt to dissuade me from a continuing friendship with Tom, who was twelve years older than I, he disclosed a previous failed marriage. When my father was nineteen, he met a woman ten years his senior, whom he later married. However there was much deception on her part, and this resulted in divorce proceedings instigated by my father. No doubt this also left him with a profound distrust of women.

So much distrust and so much past history had fashioned my parents' way of thinking. Their regret, disappointment, and recrimination had transferred itself into a crippling, limiting environment for me.

I could never understand why my life became the centre of so much negative anticipation, but as I reflect on the background and experiences my parents shared, their anxiousness for my well-being becomes more understandable.

However, after their unjust accusations had pushed me away from them, and I had abandoned my home to become a nanny when I was sixteen, there was no easy way back.

Once my diagnosis had been made, questioning its veracity proved futile. There was no emphasis on—or belief in—recovery. Instead, constant reinforcement of the need for psychiatric drugs was all I ever heard. Coming off long-term medication was never even considered.

Part One of *From the Inside of the Keyhole* demonstrates that my actions opposing the diagnosis only served to confirm it in the eyes of onlookers and professionals. Although lithium is not physically addictive, on withdrawal or reduction, one's body has to adjust to the absence of a chemical it has become used to being present, and this may be symptomatic in itself.

Part Two illustrates that accepting the diagnosis led to the belief that lithium should be able to prevent further relapses. Because I was always on such high levels of lithium, taking extra lithium during periods of stress produced the toxic effect of confusion. Practically, this led to the manifestation of 'bizarre events'.

Part Three shows that these high doses of lithium were causative to the psychosis it was employed to alleviate. Only by lowering the medication at my own instigation was I finally able to cease it completely with a positive result.

During my years of struggle, I was repeatedly hospitalized, where I suffered the devastating effects of high levels of lithium at toxic levels of up to 1.7 in combination with high levels of anti-psychotic medication. Surely a more cautious approach is needed in the administering of psychiatric medication. A realistic appraisal of the benefits and adverse effects would allow for better-informed decisions. Indeed, this would be a privilege for any patient.

My experiences also stress the importance of independent mental health advocacy—having a specialist worker represent your own feelings and viewpoint and ensure that alternative therapies are considered, and that ceasing psychiatric medication with the help of trained professionals is also a valid option, if that is the patient's decision.

As I complete this summary, Ben and I have been living in Wales for fourteen months. It is eighteen years since my last hospital admission, and over three years have passed since I ceased taking lithium. My health and fitness remain at optimum levels.

What have I learned that may be of benefit to others?

- Good communication, confronting the issues, and taking responsibility for your own actions are all prerequisites for a healthy mind-set.
- Having information withheld or never mentioned prevents rational discussion and causes disharmony.
- Reflecting on your own shortcomings and taking steps to change your approach in similar situations in the future will bring you that elusive peace of mind.
- Accepting that there are life lessons to be learnt by everyone and not just yourself redresses the balance and helps restore the harmony in your soul.

Once you have addressed the above issues:

- Physical work during the day, or half an hour on the exercise bike in the evening, can be very beneficial in inducing sleep.

- Thinking things through works well to put your life in perspective and equalize your feelings, but don't let yourself do it all night.
- Take charge of your thoughts, lie still, listen to your breathing, and let yourself dream.
- If you're still awake at two in the morning, take two soluble aspirins and believe it will let you drift off to sleep, and it will.
- Having someone you care about believe in you is the greatest inspiration to overcoming obstacles blocking your achievement. The support of such a person is very empowering—but if you don't have that good fortune, having faith in yourself and reinforcing this with positive affirmations will stand you in good stead.

Coming off lithium has been an exhilarating experience for me and has left me with a happy anticipation of my life to come and an acceptance of all that has gone before.

I am grateful to my parents for always being there in spite of everything and for instilling in me the determination and perseverance to finally free myself from the use of all psychiatric drugs, and for the fortitude to develop strategies to remain well.

Love's garden may be tended by tears, and as all the hidden truths come to light, our family garden is blossoming!

It has been said that success is not measured by what you achieve but by the obstacles you have overcome in the process. I fought against the negative expectations and made gigantic steps forward, defying my mother's constantly-reinforced beliefs that I would never be able to leave home and I would never be able to work.

I definitely proved that wasn't the case.

After completing my matriculation studies by correspondence, I attended university and achieved a bachelor of arts with a double major in psychology. After a further year of postgraduate study, I became a registered teacher in early childhood (birth to eight years). For fifteen years, I worked as a childcare director in both private and community centres with up to seventy-five children in a centre.

During my time as director, I felt my life experiences gave me an excellent understanding and empathy for people in a wide range of different and sometimes difficult situations. Both parents and staff benefited from this, and I was rewarded with many lasting friendships. I always enjoyed a warm rapport with the children as well, maintaining the ability 'see through the eyes of a child', as childhood had also been one of the happiest periods in my own life.

All of these achievements followed after Bobby and Karen allowed me the safe haven of their home when I commenced my university studies at thirty-five years of age.

After five years together, in November 2005, Benjamin and I were married in the United Welsh Church, the same church I had attended twenty years previously with Jo. Ours continues to be a very happy marriage. Benjamin has the strength and solidarity to allow me to be myself, and every day this bond of love and trust grows stronger. His practical skills, cheerful disposition, and willingness to help others set him aside as one of those outstanding people who is valued and admired by many.

Ironically, the minister from the Welsh Church who performed the marriage ceremony was the same chaplain I had befriended at Barrett Centre, and for whom I had played the organ during his Sunday services.

Being freed from the psychiatric system was perhaps my biggest triumph. A life journey that led to the lowering and finally ceasing of all psychiatric medication also gave me emancipation from any more bizarre events.

Fears of being incarcerated in a mental institution on a recurrent basis are now a dim memory. Only in dreams am I sometimes transported back to those times when my main interest was in escape, and my reflections were 'from the inside of the keyhole'.

My family general practitioner, Dr Johnson, made the comment that I could never have made these achievements and stayed symptom free over such a long period if I really had manic depression, and that my experiences would make me a better person.

Could it be that simple?

I believe that our family, friends, workmates, people we love and who have loved us, plus the environment in which we live, have far more impact on our mental health than any genetic predisposition we may inherit.

We all express ourselves in different ways, and other people's interpretation of our expression is merely their viewpoint.

You have read some of the snippets from my life, and maybe this will influence your way of thinking about your own actions and the actions of those close to you.

You must always believe in yourself no matter what.

About the Author

Author Margaret Griffiths worked as a director in childcare centres for her last fifteen years in Australia and was a registered teacher of early childhood (from birth to eight years). Although qualified with a bachelor of arts with a double major in psychology, the author penned *From the Inside of the Keyhole* from personal experience.

She now lives with her husband, Benjamin, his brother Vyrnwy and their two Jack Russell dogs, Marshall and Maxwell, in the small village of Aberarad, just outside Newcastle Emlyn in Wales in the United Kingdom.

From the Inside of the Keyhole is available for purchase through Google and Amazon search programmes. The author may be contacted on bemarwyn@gmail.com and welcomes any queries, feedback or reviews.

Lightning Source UK Ltd.
Milton Keynes UK
UKOW041001290513

211421UK00002B/34/P